Published by Collins Educational
An imprint of HarperCollinsPublishers Ltd
77-85 Fulham Palace Road
London W6 8JB

The HarperCollins website address is www.fireandwater.com
© HarperCollinsPublishers Ltd 1999
First published 1999
ISBN 0 00 322491 0

Mundher Adhami, Jean Cheshire, Christine Collins, Mark Pepper and
Anne White assert the moral right to be identified as the authors of this work.

British Library Cataloguing in Publication Data
A catalogue record for this book is available from the British Library.

Edited by Dodi Beardshaw
Picture research by Caroline Thompson
Design by Chi Leung
Commissioning Editor: Alison Walters
Cover photographs: Tony Stone Images
Illustrations by Barking Dog Art, Russell Birkett, Bethan Matthews and Harry Venning
Production by Anna Pauletti
Printed and bound by Scotprint, Musselburgh.

Acknowledgements

Every effort has been made to contact the holders of copyright material, but if any have
been inadvertently overlooked the publishers will be pleased to make the necessary
arrangements at the first opportunity.

The publishers would like to thank the following for permission to reproduce photographs
(T = Top, B = Bottom, C = Centre, L= Left, R = Right):

Allsport/Hulton Deutsch, 37, G Chadwick, 55, A Livesey, 84;
M Wagner/Aviation Images, 77;
BBC Picture Archives Photograph Library, 106;
John Birdsall Photography, 48R, 50, 80R;
Blackpool Gazette/D Nelson, 104;
Shield, 1998 (acrylic on board) by Peter H Mcclure, Private Collection/Bridgeman
Art Library, London, 110;
J Allan Cash Ltd, 93;
A Bacchella/Bruce Coleman Ltd, 48CR;
Creative Comics, 22;
Leslie Garland, 30TR, 96;
Ronald Grant Archive, 9;
Andrew Lambert, 6, 17, 23, 30TL, 33, 41B, 42, 48L&CL, 72TL, 82;
P Reynolds/Frank Lane Picture Agency, 124;
London Aerial Photo Library, 43;
Polydron International Ltd, 115;
QA Photos/NMEC, 69;
Redferns/K Doherty, 39, P Ford, 67;
Rex Features Ltd, 24, 41T, 72CL, 99;
Gavin Rowe, 72R;
Tony Stone Images, 35, 65, 74, 88, 112, 121;
Telegraph Colour Library, 102;
Illustrations from WHERE'S WALLY? © 1987 Martin Handford. Reproduced by kind
permission of the publisher Walker Books Ltd, 32;
John Walmsley, 19, 30C, 45, 53, 76, 80L, 86.

Module B1

Number and money

1 Reading money
Reading and writing amounts of money in figures and words

2 Counting money
Counting any amount of money using coins and notes. Recognising when there is enough money to meet a price

3 Making up an amount
Choosing appropriately from a collection of coins and notes (or other forms, e.g. stamps and vouchers) to make up a given sum. Recognising when an exact equivalent is not possible and dealing with the exchange

4 Giving the right change
Giving change for any amount. Recognising when enough coins are available to make the change. Finding ways of making the exchange feasible when change is short

5 Approximate costs
Stating the very approximate cost of items regularly purchased. Knowing that there may be a range of possible responses

6 Money skills
Using and applying skills in handling money problems in a mixed setting

Key words and phrases

amount
change
figures
value

approximate
counting on
place value
range
rough
rounded
skip count

coin
note
pence
pounds
stamp
tokens
voucher

① Reading money

How many items can you see that cost more than £4?

Say the following amounts.
1. £2.68
2. £5.16
3. £4.02
4. £8.40
5. Make the same amounts using place value cards.
6. Write these amounts in words.

Work in pairs. The first person says amount **a**. The second says amount **b**.
If you think your partner is saying it wrongly check with your teacher.

	a		b			a		b
1	£2.89	b	£3.76		6	£8.20	b	£8.16
2	£5.46	b	£7.62		7	£7.15	b	£6.13
3	£6.41	b	£1.53		8	£6.04	b	£7.08
4	£8.37	b	£4.58		9	£5.30	b	£6.20
5	£7.25	b	£3.27		10	£4.75	b	£5.95

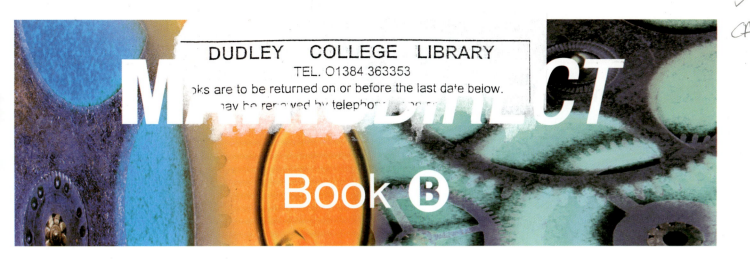

MATHS DIRECT

Book B

Jean Cheshire
Christine Collins
Mark Pepper
Anne White

Series Editor: **Mundher Adhami**

Collins Educational

An imprint of HarperCollins Publishers

Contents

C

Collect a full set of place value cards and make the following amounts.

1. five pounds forty-two
2. six pounds eighty-three
3. two pounds sixty-four
4. nine pounds thirty-seven
5. one pound ninety-two
6. four pounds sixteen
7. nine pounds seventeen
8. two pounds thirteen
9. three pounds ten
10. two pounds five

D

Write the amounts shown here in figures.

1 

2 

3 

4 

5 

6 

7 

8 

9 

10 

E

Match the item to its price in words. Two are done for you.

1 eighteen pounds ninety-nine   *Radio*
2 seventeen pounds twenty-five
3 twelve pounds seventy-nine
4 thirty-two pounds and five pence
5 nine pounds ninety-nine
6 ten pounds fifty
7 sixty-seven pounds and nine pence
8 seventy-five pounds ninety
9 nine pounds forty-nine   *Walkman*
10 twelve pounds forty-nine
11 five pounds ninety-nine
12 twenty-one pounds fifty
13 eight pounds fifty
14 thirteen pounds ninety-nine

Now look back at your work in this lesson.
• Can you read and write amounts of money in numbers?
• Do you know how to read the pence parts when there is only one digit?

② Counting money

Here is Scrooge counting his money.
How often do you think he does this?

Answer the following questions.

1 Count the money shown here.

2 Count out the notes and coins needed to pay this bill.

Trousers	£	15.99
Blouse	£	12.00
Minimum payment of £10.00 to reach us by 12.03.99	Total £	39.47

3 What is the smallest number of notes and coins which could be used to pay this bill?

3 fruit salads	£	3.60
Coffee for three	£	3.00
Service included	Total £	17.24

4 Here are Karen's savings. How much more does she need to save to buy the radio-cassette player?

£89

Count the money shown here.

| 1 | 3 | 5 |
| 2 | 4 | 6 |

Write down or draw the notes and coins needed to pay the following bills.

1 £35.60   4 £90.07
2 £85.70   5 £88.21
3 £46.63   6 £61.14

Which of these piles of money are the same as each other?

| 1 | 3 | 5 |
| 2 | 4 | 6 |

You must pay these bills with as few coins and notes as possible.
Draw or list the money you use.

1 £13.70   4 £26.89
2 £86.45   5 £34.61
3 £52.38   6 £49.99

A school ski trip costs £100. Count each of these piles of money
and say how much more each pupil must save to go on the trip.

Now look back at your work in this lesson.
- Can you count any amount of money in coins and notes?
- Do you know when there is enough money to meet a price
  and when there isn't?

❸ Making up an amount

This customer is short of money. What could happen now?

Answer the following questions.

1 Which of these stamps should be put on this letter?

2 Has Sally got enough petrol vouchers for a personal stereo?

3 How many items can Anil choose from the sweet counter for 50p?

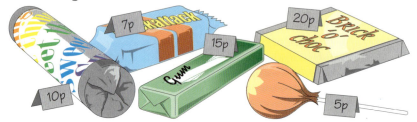

4 Mira exchanges an expensive hairdryer for a simpler one. She is given vouchers to cover the difference in price. Which vouchers should the assistant give her?

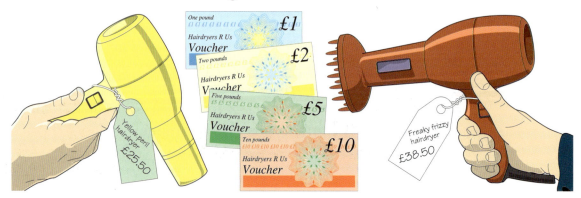

B Simon has a part-time job helping at his Mum's office. He has to sort and stamp the post. Here are the stamps he has. Each letter has been weighed and the correct stamp value is written on it. He must not waste money so he looks for the closest combination of stamps he can find. Which stamps should he put on each letter?

C Mel's gran has been saving stamps for her bills. She asks Melanie to pay for her at the post office. Which bills can she pay using the stamps her gran has given her? Which bills can't she pay?

1 Phone £28.56

2 Gas £45.69

3 Electricity £26.78

4 TV licence £89.50

D

This snack machine does not give change.

| A1 | 12p | B1 | 15p | C1 | 25p | A2 | 34p | B2 | 38p |

Anil and his friends decide to try to get as many different snacks as they can for their money. What should they choose if:

1 Anil puts in 50p?
2 Angela puts in £1?
3 Mira puts in three 20p pieces?
4 Damien puts in 50p and 20p?

E

Habib has these tokens.

He looks at the prices of CDs in his local record shop.

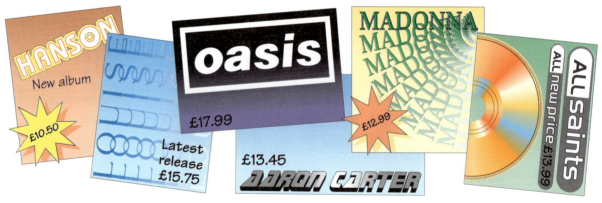

HANSON New album £10.50
Latest release £15.75
oasis £17.99
£13.45 AARON CARTER
MADONNA £12.99
ALL SAINTS ALL new price £13.99

Which tokens should he use to buy these CDs?
1 All Saints and Madonna
2 Oasis, Madonna and Hanson
3 Aaron Carter and Louise
4 Louise and Madonna
5 Aaron Carter, Louise and Madonna

Now look back at your work in this lesson.
- Can you count the right notes and coins for any amount?
- Do you know when you have enough money to pay for something?

④ Giving the right change

The shopkeeper gave back 43p in change. What is the customer saying?

 Answer the following questions.

1 Which two piles of coins would go together to make a pound?

a   b   c   d   e

2 Chian has paid £1. Has she been given the correct change?

75p

3 What change should be given from a £2 coin for these items?

37p   52p

4 Can these coins be used to give change from £1 for the following?

34p

22p

 Match the pairs of piles of coins which add together to make a pound.

 1    3   5   7   9

 2   4   6   8   10

C

Michelle takes her little sisters and their friends to the shop. They each have a £1 coin to spend. When they get home Michelle checks the bills and the change. Who has been given the wrong change?

	Kelly 68p	Laura 81p	Olivia 47p	Anna 54p	Lucy 61p
	1 32p	**2** 29p	**3** 53p	**4** 46p	**5** 38p

D

Marcus is in charge of the pet stall at the school fair. What change should he give to customers if each of them gives him £1?

1 83p   **2** 41p   **3** 67p   **4** 14p

E

Marcus asks his customers for help with the shortage of copper. Alice buys a cat comb at 37p and offers a £1 coin. He asks her for another 7p and then gives her 70p change. He explains by counting on from 37p to £1.07.

47, 57, 67, 77, 87, 97, 107

1 What extra coins should Marcus ask for when his next four customers want to buy the following things?

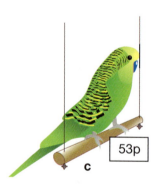

a   35p   b   64p   c   53p   d   72p

2 Write what he counts out loud as he gives these customers their change in 10p coins.

Now look back at your work in this lesson.
- Can you give change from a £1 and £2 coin?
- Do you know what to do if you do not have the right coins to give the right change?

❺ Approximate costs

Which of the things in the photo were the most expensive when bought new? Which were the cheapest?

Answer the following questions.

1 Which item belongs to which price ticket?

a   b   c   d

£1.04

21p

87p

99p

2 Which of these items is most likely to cost less than £5?

a   b   c   d   e   f

3 What is the rough cost of a sweatshirt?

4 What is the rough cost of a regular size bar of chocolate?

5 What is the rough cost of a magazine?

Josie is helping her aunt make a window display in her village shop. She must place the correct tickets with the goods. Which price goes with which item?

£6.99
£1.25
£3.75
65p
£13.50
£59.99
£19.99

C This week all the items costing less than £1 are to be put on display in the shop window.
Which of these items should go in the window?

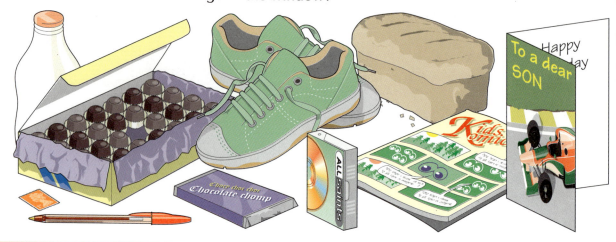

D What is the approximate cost of these items?

1 pair of trainers
2 single pop CD
3 bar of chocolate
4 bag of crisps
5 small bottle of drink
6 cinema ticket

E These price tickets have been mixed up. Can you sort them out?

Now look back at your work in this lesson.
- Do you know roughly the prices of things you buy often?
- Do you know when the shop price of something is too expensive or too cheap?

6 Money skills

This girl felt generous and gave roughly half of the coins in her pocket.

Estimate how much you have in your pocket or purse without counting, then check. How near were you? to the penny? to the nearest 10p? to the nearest £1?

Give these amounts in words.

1 £4.72

2 £2.06

3 £3.30

4 How much money is here in total?

Answer the following questions.

1 These are the only stamps in the office. How many of these stamps should Paul put on a package if the scales tell him it should cost £1.32?

2 How much change should be given from a £1 coin for a bunch of grapes costing 67p?

3 Roughly how much does a can of fizzy drink cost?

Give these amounts in words.

1 £3.87

2 £0.56

3 £4.08

4 £9.60

5 £7.14

Write these amounts in figures.

6 five pounds and two pence

7 seven pounds eighteen

8 six pounds thirty

9 nine pounds ninety-nine

10 four pounds thirty-one

D Year 7 have been helping on a charity day. They empty their tins back at school and there is a prize for the person who collected the most. Write down how much each person collected and say who wins the prize.

5 Salma

3 Josie

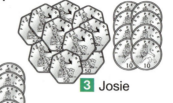
4 Maria

1 Jack

2 Habib

E A holiday booking gives Mira's family the following vouchers to use during their stay at the Ski Centre. Which tokens should they use at these attractions?

Ski Centre 2 TOKEN	Ski Centre 5 TOKEN	Ski Centre 10 TOKEN	Ski Centre 50 TOKEN	Ski Centre 100 TOKEN
Ski Centre 2 TOKEN	Ski Centre 5 TOKEN	Ski Centre 10 TOKEN	Ski Centre 50 TOKEN	
Ski Centre 2 TOKEN	Ski Centre 5 TOKEN	Ski Centre 10 TOKEN		
Ski Centre 2 TOKEN	Ski Centre 5 TOKEN	Ski Centre 10 TOKEN		
Ski Centre 2 TOKEN	Ski Centre 5 TOKEN	Ski Centre 10 TOKEN		
	Ski Centre 5 TOKEN			
	Ski Centre 5 TOKEN			
	Ski Centre 5 TOKEN			

CENTRE POOL
Family admission
19 tokens
1

Ski hire: 68 tokens
3

Take the family on a tour of the mountains for only
84 tokens
5

Why not try the famous
Mountain View Cafe
Family meals: 42 tokens
2

Family ski lift pass
27 Tokens
4

F Mark takes a £1 coin to school each day for shopping on his way home. How much change should he get after buying each of these things?

CHOC BAR 27p
1

Sparky's Crisps cheese & onion 18p 15% EXTRA
2

BANANA MILKSHAKE 48p
3

slush Ice 63p
4

OFF ROAD MONTHLY MAGAZINE 72p
5

Now look back at your work in this lesson.
- Do you think it is easier to give change from a pound than to count how much money you have?
- Apart from coins, what else can you use to buy things with?

Module B2

Handling data

❶ Collecting data in a system
Recording information about people or things in an organised way

❷ Personal measurements
Knowing your own sizes such as shoes and clothes and also facts such as your full name, address and date of birth

❸ How much does it really hold?
Knowing when bottles or other containers that look similar actually hold a different amount of liquid. Finding ways to know which of two containers holds more than the other

❹ Height is not everything
Being able to say which containers of the same make are bigger or smaller than others by looking not only at the height but also at other measures

❺ Measuring how much things hold
Knowing what things are measured in millilitres (or cubic centimetres), litres and cubic metres

❻ Data and measurement skills
Revising and practising skills and knowledge about containers and personal measurements

Key words and phrases

capacity
data
depth
dimensions
height
length
measure
measurements
volume
width

collect
compare
count
estimate
sort

cubic centimetre
cubic metre
Euro and UK sizing
gallon
litre
measuring jug
millilitre
pint
sizes
units of measurement

① Collecting data in a system

Which of these cartoon words has more vowels than consonants? Which has the same number of each? Make up a cartoon word of your own.

Cartoon characters often use nonsense words that have more vowels than consonants. Look at the words in the picture above.

1. How many times can you find the letter 'a' in the two sentences above?
2. How many 'e's are there?
3. How many 'i's, 'o's and 'u's can be found?
4. Which vowel is used most frequently?
5. What is the total number of vowels used altogether? You may use a calculator.
6. Do you think the number of vowels is more than half the total number of letters?

Jake collected data from his class by asking the pupils which was their favourite sport. He made a tally table with his results.

Sport	Votes	Total
Cricket	✓✓✓✓	
Football	✓✓✓✓✓✓✓✓	
Hockey	✓✓	
Tennis	✓✓✓✓✓	
Athletics	✓✓✓	
Swimming	✓✓✓✓✓	

1. Copy the table into your book and fill in the totals. Look at Jake's table and find the following.
2. Which sport was the most popular?
3. Which two sports scored the same number of votes?
4. One sport got twice as many votes as athletics. Which was it?
5. How many pupils did Jake ask for his tally table?

Find out the birthday months of your classmates.

1 Make a table of the months of the year with columns for your classmates' names and the total.

2 Write each person's name against the month they were born.

3 When you have finished find the total for each month.

4 Which month has the most people in it?

5 Which month has the fewest people or none?

6 Do you think another class would have the same kind of data?

Month	Names	Total
January		
February		

Jim has fallen ill with a strange illness. The doctor says he should remove all metal and plastic objects from his room for a while. He can keep wooden objects and things made from textiles.

1 Make a table like the one below of the objects you can recognise in the room. Put the objects in the first column. In the second column write which material each object is made of. List at least ten objects in your table.

Object	Material

2 For each object write down whether it is made of metal, wood, plastic, or textiles. If you are not sure write 'Not sure'.

3 Now make another table like this.

4 In the second column fill in all the objects made from each material. Use the information from your first table. Now complete the last column with the totals.

5 How many of the objects in your list will Jim have to remove from the room?

Material	Objects	Totals
Metal		
Wood		
Plastic		
Textiles		
Not sure		

Now look back at your work in this lesson.
- Can you record information about people or things in an organised way?
- Which way do you like to record information the best?

2 Personal measurements

One of the people in this picture is the tallest man in the world.
Which one?
Do you know what size shoe you take?

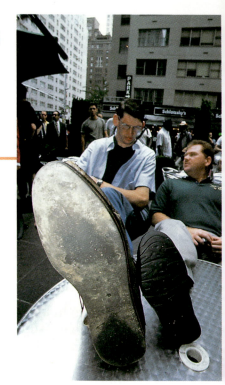

 Azeem was born in 1985 during March on the 17th day of the month. His date of birth can be written in two ways. The first way is:

17th March 1985

The second and shorter way is:

17.3.85

1 Write your own date of birth the long way.
2 Now write it the short way.
3 Write down your age in years and months.
4 Write down your height the last time you have measured it.
5 Write down your weight the last time you weighed yourself.

 Azeem's address is:

45, High Street,
Branley,
Frenshire,
BR7 654

1 Write your full name.
2 Write your address in the same way as Azeem's.
3 Write the address of one of your friends in the same way.
4 Write the school's address in the same way.

 You need to buy a new jacket for school.
1 Decide which length you would prefer from the pictures here.

Short

Regular

Long

2 Where would you need to measure from to find the right length: your neck, or your waist?
3 Using a tape measure, help each other find how long your jacket needs to be.
4 Write your measurement in inches, to the nearest inch.
5 Write it again in centimetres, to the nearest centimetre.

Women's clothes are measured in different ways around the world.

Waist measurements	UK sizes	US sizes	European sizes
24 inches	8	4	34
25 inches	10	6	36
27 inches	12	8	38
29 inches	14	10	40
31 inches	16	12	42

1 Rebecca has gone to France for a day trip to do some shopping. She wants to buy a new pair of jeans. In the UK, she would buy a size 10. What size would she buy in France?

2 Zoë's cousin has sent her a T-shirt from New York. The T-shirt is a US size 10. Zoë is a UK size 10. What size should Zoë's cousin have sent?

3 Lucia has a waist measurement of 27 inches. What is her UK size?

4 What is Lucia's waist measurement in centimetres?

5 Tina is a European size 40, Gill is a US size 6. Which girl has the larger size?

Shoes have a UK and a Euro size.

1 What size shoes do you take?

2 What size is this in Euro sizing? Use the table to help you.

UK sizes	Euro sizes	UK sizes	Euro sizes
3	36	7	41
4	37	8	42
5	38	9	43
6	39	10	44
6½	40	11	45

3 Why is it more important to know your exact size of shoe rather than most other items of clothing?

Now look back at your work in this lesson.
- Do you know your own sizes of shoes and clothes?
- Can you quickly write your full name, address and date of birth if need be?

③ How much does it really hold?

These three bottles look the same size from the outside but they hold different amounts of liquid. The wizard can tell which bottle holds the most with his x-ray vision. Which one do you think it is?

Will they guess this is a trick bottle?

Christopher has three jugs – a blue one, a red one and a green one. He fills the blue jug with water and empties it into the green one. He finds that there is not enough water to fill the green jug.

1 Which jug holds the most water?

2 If he filled the green jug and emptied it into the blue one what would happen?

He fills both jugs with water and then empties them both into a red jug without spilling any!

3 Which jug holds the most water: the blue, the green or the red?

4 List the three jugs in order starting with the largest capacity.

Ms McDuff has two flower vases which are too tall to fit under the tap in the kitchen. She fills them with a mug which she fills with water and empties into them until they are full.

The vase with the roses on takes seven mugs and the vase with the daffodils on takes ten.

1 Which is the larger vase?

1 How many more mugs of water does the larger vase hold?

3 If she has put six mugs of water into each vase how many more will the rose vase need?

4 How many more will the daffodil vase need?

C

Saima has a large bottle of lemonade and a small bottle of fizzy water. She also has a packet of plastic glasses.
She can fill eight glasses from one bottle and four from the other.

1 Which bottle did she fill the eight glasses with?
2 Which bottle did she fill the four glasses with?
3 If she bought another small bottle of fizzy water, how many glasses could she fill altogether?

D

Frank is painting the garage. He has two empty containers, **a** and **b**. He wants to find out which will hold the most paint to save him having to fill it too often from the paint tin.

1 Would it be sensible for him to pour paint from one container to the other? How does that help him find which is bigger?
2 He is in the kitchen. What could he use to help him find out before he opens the paint?
3 Explain how you would do this.

E

Carla's little sisters are making a sandcastle on the beach.
Jodie makes the large sand pies and Ella makes small ones.

Ella   Jodie

1 Which sister's bucket holds the most sand?
2 Which one has to put the least sand in her bucket?
3 Which bucket will be heavier when it is full?
4 Both girls have the same size spade and one bucket holds twice as much sand as the other.
Jodie's bucket holds ten spades full. How many does Ella's hold?

Now look back at your work in this lesson.
- Are you surprised when bottles that look similar, sometimes hold different amounts of liquid?
- Do you know a good way to find out which of two bottles holds more liquid?

④ Height is not everything

Each month Sam has to clean the tank without moving it. He empties out the water using a jug and a shallow bowl, and puts the old water in a bucket.

Look at the picture of Sam and his fishtank.

1. Why can't Sam empty the water from the tank straight into the bucket?
2. Which is easier to use in emptying the water, the jug or the bowl?
3. When does Sam use the shallow bowl?
4. Can you guess by just looking that the bowl holds about as much water as the jug? How can you explain this?

These fish tanks are only partly full.

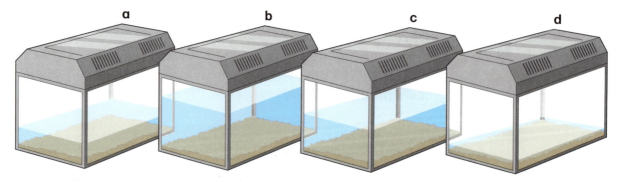

Which picture shows a tank with:

1. One jug of water?
2. Four jugs of water?
3. 8 jugs of water?
4. 12 jugs of water?

Look at this bucket and this jug, and at the fish tanks in exercise B.

1 Can you tell just by looking that eight jugs of water fill the bucket? How can you explain this?

2 Which holds the most water, the tank or the bucket?

3 How can you tell from the picture that it takes two buckets to fill a tank?

4 How many jugs of water does the tank hold?

5 How many times did Sam fill the jug with the water from the tank?

Sam's mum has dug a square hole in the garden to make a fishpond. When he measures it he finds that it does not hold enough water for all his fish. If she makes the hole deeper or the edges higher it will be difficult to clean it.

1 What should she do to the pond to make it hold more water?

2 If she makes it twice as long how much more water will it hold?

3 If she makes it wider will it hold more or less?

4 She took 20 minutes to fill the first small pond with a hose pipe. How long will it take to fill the one that is twice as long?

5 If she then makes this one twice as wide as well what can you say about the filling time?

Look at this collection of containers.

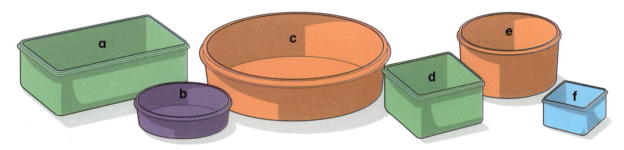

1 Which one holds the most liquid: **a** or **b**? Give a reason for your answer.

2 Does container **c** hold more or less than **d**?

3 Put the containers in order of capacity.

4 Container **e** and **f** both fit on my shelf. Which one will hold the most sugar?

5 Can you explain why?

Now look back at your work in this lesson.
- How can two bottles that have the same height hold different amounts of water?
- What things, apart from height, do you look for when you are deciding which bottle is bigger?

⑤ Measuring how much things hold

Cement is used to fill in holes, so it is normally measured in volume, not in weight. The giant cement mixer can make 20 cubic metres of cement in one go, enough to fill half a room.

The small cement mixer will make a smaller amount, about 100 litres. You could fill it with about a hundred average-size bottles. It could make enough cement for a step in front of the house.

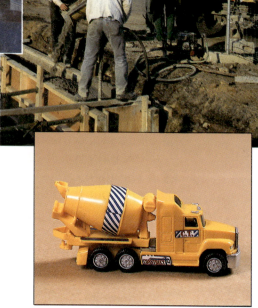

The toy cement mixer can hold a small cup of water, about 100 cubic centimetres or cc for short. These are also called millilitres, or ml for short.

Write down how these things will be measured: in cubic metres, litres or cubic centimetres.

1 A bottle of perfume
2 Oil tanker at sea
3 Petrol you put in the car
4 Water flowing in a small river per hour
5 Can of soup
6 Soil sold at the garden centre, enough for a new garden

There are 1000 cc or ml in one litre.
How many ml are there in the following?

1 2 litres
2 5 litres
3 10 litres
4 7 litres
5 one and a half litres
6 three and a half litres
7 five and a half litres
8 one and a quarter litres

C

Which of the following containers is most likely to fit these measures?

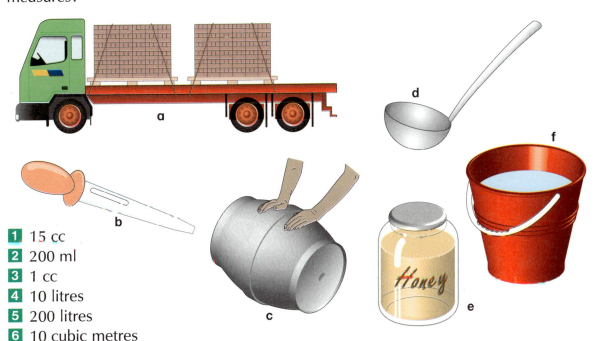

1. 15 cc
2. 200 ml
3. 1 cc
4. 10 litres
5. 200 litres
6. 10 cubic metres

D

In the past people used other measures such as gallons and pints.
Some of these are still used, and you can see them written on things.
A pint is a bit more than half a litre.
A gallon is a bit more than four litres.

1. Can you think of two or more things that were, or still are, measured in pints?
2. Can you think of two or more things that were, or still are, measured in gallons?

Now look back at your work in this lesson.
- Do you know what things are measured in millilitres (or cubic centimetres)? How do you write these measurements in a short form?
- Do you know what things are measured in pints or litres?

⑥ Data and measurement skills

Can you find Wally in this picture?
He's got a stripey jumper on.
Can you see any other stripey jumpers?

Wally
©1987 Martin Handford

Systematic recording

1 Copy this table and do the tally marks and totals needed from the picture. Look at one part of the picture at a time.

	Tally	Total
A man		
A woman		
A hat		
A child		
An animal		
A handbag		

Height measurements

John is 158 cm tall, Mary is 162 cm, Sasha is 167 cm and Peter is 169 cm.

1 Which pupil is the tallest?

2 Who is taller than John but shorter than Sasha?

3 Who is taller than Mary but shorter than Peter?

4 Which pupil would you expect to have the smallest feet?

5 Could you be certain without finding out?

Compare capacities

Bag A holds 5 kg of potatoes, Sack B contains 20 kg and Box C is empty.

1 How many of Bag A could you fill from Sack B?

2 Box C will hold three sacks of potatoes. How many kg of potatoes does the box hold?

3 How many bags of potatoes could be filled from the box?

D

Capacity dimensions

1 Can the two containers **a** and **b** hold roughly the same amount of water?

2 Why are containers that can hold the same amount made in such different forms?

3 How many of container **b** will fill container **c**?

4 How many of container **a** will fill container **c**?

E

Measures for capacity

d A large spoon

j

a

b
Beer drinking

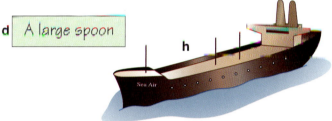
e Large piles of building bricks

h Ink cartridge of a pen

c

g TOMATO SOUP

k MILK SEMI-SKIMMED

i Jars of jam and honey

Which things can be:

1 measured in millilitres
2 measured in litres
3 measured in cubic metres
4 measured in pints
5 measured in gallons

Now look back at your work in this lesson.
- Can you decide by looking at two containers which one is bigger?
- Which mathematical words in this lesson do you now understand better?

Module **B**3

Number and algebra

❶ Numbers in the mind

Knowing when to add or take away numbers. When the numbers are small adding and taking away without pen and paper or calculator

❷ Repeat adding or repeat taking away

Keeping track of numbers when you add numbers more than once, or when you take away numbers more than once

❸ Two-digit numbers

Practising and talking about your mental methods of adding or taking away numbers

❹ Repeat measures

When something is much bigger than the unit of measure then you can repeat measuring and keep track of it

❺ About how long?

Knowing about how long is a metre and a centimetre, and using these to estimate lengths

❻ Mind skills with numbers

Revising mental work with numbers, repeated addition and taking away, repeated measuring and knowing the size of centimetres and metres

Key words and phrases

add on
altogether
continue
count on
in n days' time
n days ago
repeat adding
repeat taking away

centimetre
diagonal
length
measure
metre
perimeter
width

① Numbers in the mind

Do you ever shop at a market rather than at the shops?
Why do you think prices are normally cheaper at a market than in the shops?
What other kinds of markets are there?

If prices at a market are increased by 6p on all items, what will the new prices be?

		Old price	New price
1	1 lb onions	18p	
2	1 lb carrots	21p	
3	1 lb parsnips	??p	
4	5 lb potatoes	54p	
5	Cabbage	50p	
6	Cauliflower	45p	

Answer these questions.
Work them out in your head.

1 17 + 6 =   4 42 + 7 =
2 22 + 8 =   5 55 + 6 =
3 29 + 8 =   6 79 + 5 =

Imagine today's date is 12 July. Work out the dates of the following events.

1 Simon's birthday is in nine days' time.
2 Five days ago, the school went on a trip to the seaside.
3 The last day of term is in seven days' time.
4 The swimming gala is in four days' time.
5 Ten days ago was parents' evening.
6 Samantha is going to buy a kitten in three days' time.

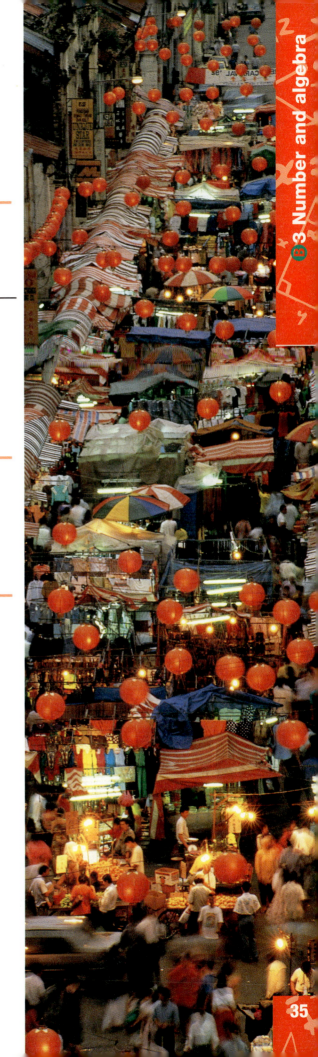

D

Chantelle and her friends are playing a special game of darts. Each player starts with a score of 20 and has to try to reduce their score to exactly 0. The first player to do this is the winner. Each player throws three darts. Add up their scores.

1 Chantelle   5 + 5 + 4
2 Bernadette   4 + 3 + 9
3 Moshud   8 + 8 + 4
4 Harshad   16 + 2 + 1
5 Fatima   3 + 5 + 7
6 Who is the winner?

E

A breakfast cereal has a special offer. Ten tokens can be exchanged for a book.

Work out in your head how many tokens each of the pupils have now.

Then work out and write down how many more tokens each pupil needs to get the prize.

1 Mandy	Large	Small	Small	
2 Winston	Large	Large		
3 Clare	Small	Small		
4 Melissa	Medium	Small	Small	Small
5 Bill	Small	Medium	Medium	Small
6 Harry	Large	Medium	Medium	Small

Now look back at your work in this lesson.
- Do you know how to add numbers, and can you do this in your head?
- Do you know how to take away numbers in the same way?

② Repeat adding, and repeat taking away

This is Gary Sobers. By hitting 6 sixes in one over, he became a world record holder in first class cricket.
Have you ever been to a cricket match?
It is usually a lot slower than when Sobers hit his 6 sixes!

There are six balls in an over. Work out how many runs are scored in these overs.

1 0, 0, 4, 4, 4, 4
2 6, 6, 0, 6, 0, 6
3 4, 4, 4, 4, 4, 4

4 4, 4, 4, 0, 0, 4
5 6, 6, 0, 0, 6, 0
6 6, 6, 6, 6, 6, 6

Work out the following. Use the repeat function on the calculator if you want to.

1 12 + 12 + 12 + 12 + 12 + 12
2 15 + 15 + 15 + 15 + 15 + 15
3 17 + 17 + 17 + 17 + 17 + 17
4 400 - 20 - 20 - 20 - 20 - 20 - 20 - 20
5 500 - 15 - 15 - 15 - 15 - 15 - 15

Vicky is helping to get refreshments for her little sister's class party. She decides that they need six of each item. Find out the total cost by adding the cost of six of each item on your calculator or by any other way.

	Cost of one	Cost of six
1 Crisps	31p	
2 Packets of biscuits	45p	
3 Packets of nuts	32p	
4 Bottles of cola	92p	
5 Carton of cakes	82p	
6 Fun-size chocolate bars	15p	

When Vicky does the shopping for her sister's party, she uses a 'loyalty card' to earn points. Work out how many points she will earn for each of the following.

10 points
when you buy 6

5 points
when you buy 1

25 points
when you buy 2

50 points
when you buy 2

10 points
when you buy 3

1 Six cola drinks
2 Six packets of biscuits
3 Six packets of nuts
4 Six cartons of cakes
5 Six fun-size chocolate bars
6 How many points does she earn altogether?

Sayeed and his friends play darts. In darts, you can score a single, double or triple for each of the numbers 1–20. Work out the totals of their scores.

Name	Single	Double	Triple
1 Sayeed	6	18	7
2 Tracey	12	10, 14	–
3 Sean	2	5	14
4 Anna	5	–	3, 11
5 Jason	16	1, 4	–
6 Carol	7	–	14, 20

Now look back at your work in this lesson.
• Can you add the number twice or more times?
• How do you keep track of how many times you have added a number?

③ Two-digit numbers

The Top Twenty is important in pop music as it shows the 20 best-selling singles. What is Number 1 at the moment? What do you think will be Number 1 next week?

Work out the position in the Top Twenty of these singles. If they move Down you add the numbers, when Up you take away.

Present position	Move up or down	New position
1 4	Down 6	
2 18	Up 12	
3 20	Up 6	
4 1	Down 7	
5 15	Up 13	
6 8	Up 7	

Write down six different ways of adding coins so that they total exactly 20p. You do not have to use all the coins.

Write the answers to these questions.

1 20 - 4
2 20 - 11
3 30 - 16
4 20 - 20
5 20 - 18
6 40 - 5

D Twenty people travel on a train that has just three carriages.

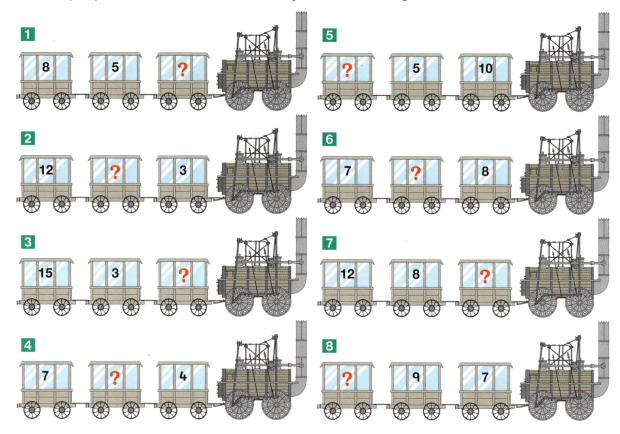

How many people travel in each unmarked carriage?

E Copy each of these questions into your book with two square boxes for the dice opposite each one. Draw the dots on the blank dice to make correct sums. If there is more than one correct answer just draw one correct sum. The first one is done for you.

1 Add up to 10

2 Add up to 9	5 Add up to 11
3 Add up to 12	6 Add up to 8
4 Add up to 5	7 Add up to 7
	8 Add up to 6

Now look back at your work in this lesson.
- Explain your method of adding or taking away numbers in your head.
- Up to what number can you add and subtract numbers in your head? 20? 30? 40? 50?

4 Repeat measures

This is the biggest pizza ever made.
What other kinds of food would you
like to see made into the 'biggest ever'?

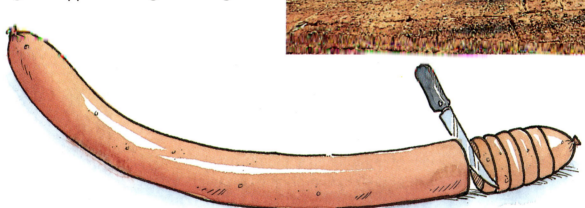

The longest sausage has to be cut up
and eaten. Suppose it is cut into equal
portions of the width of two of your
fingers – approximately 3 cm long.

Work out the overall lengths of the following number of portions.
Copy the sentences and write in the answers.
1. 8 portions will have a length of ☆ cm.
2. 10 portions will have a length of ☆ cm.
3. 12 portions will have a length of ☆ cm.
4. 15 portions will have a length of ☆ cm.
5. 18 portions will have a length of ☆ cm.
6. 20 portions will have a length of ☆ cm.

Make measurements with 'foot-lengths'. Do
this by putting one foot in front of the other,
so that the heel of one foot just touches the
toe of the other foot.

Copy these sentences and write in the answers.
1. The length of my classroom is 👣 foot-lengths.
2. The width of my classroom is 👣 foot-lengths.
3. The width of the door is 👣 foot-lengths.
4. The diagonal of my classroom is 👣 foot-lengths.
5. The perimeter of my classroom is 👣 foot-lengths.
6. How can you check if your measurement for the
   perimeter of your classroom is fairly accurate?

This time you will measure using your normal stride. The number of strides is usually known as 'paces'. Copy these sentences and write in the answers.

1 The length of my classroom is 🏃 paces.
2 The width of my classroom is 🏃 paces.
3 The width of the door is 🏃 paces.
4 The diagonal of my classroom is 🏃 paces.
5 The perimeter of my classroom is 🏃 paces
6 There are about 🏃 of my foot-lengths in one of my paces.

Now use part of your thumb as a measurement. Bend your thumb and measure with the part of the thumb that is between the knuckle and the joint. We will call these 'thumb-spans'.
Copy these sentences and write in the answers.

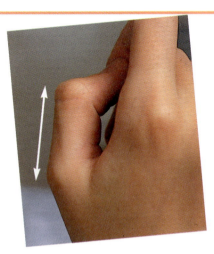

1 The length of my pencil is ▲ thumb-spans.
2 The width of my writing book is ▲ thumb-spans.
3 The length of my writing book is ▲ thumb-spans.
4 The length of my ruler is ▲ thumb-spans.
5 The width of my ruler is ▲ thumb-spans.
6 The width of my reading book is ▲ thumb-spans.

Now measure with the length of your hand. This is called a 'hand-span'.

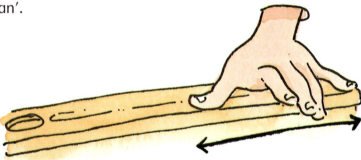

Copy these sentences and write in the answers.

1 The width of my desk is 🖐 hand-spans.
2 The length of my desk is 🖐 hand-spans.
3 The width of the door is 🖐 hand-spans.
4 The length of the metre ruler is 🖐 hand-spans.
5 The height of my chair is 🖐 hand-spans.
6 The width of a cupboard in my classroom is 🖐 hand-spans.

Now look back at your work in this lesson.
• How can you measure the length of the playground?
• How you can keep track of how many times you have used your unit of measure?

⑤ About how long?

The distance around the athletics track at Crystal Palace Stadium is 400 metres (400 m). Have you ever been to an athletics track? How long would it take you to run 400 m?

Copy these sentences and work out the answers.
1. Twice round the track is ✎ m.
2. Half-way round the track is ✎ m.
3. One-quarter of the track is ✎ m.
4. Three times round the track is ✎ m.
5. Four times round the track is ✎ m.
6. Five times round the track is ✎ m.

You will need a 30 centimetre ruler to measure your classroom. Copy these sentences and work out the answers.

1. The width of my classroom window is ✎ ruler lengths.
2. The width of the door is ✎ ruler lengths.
3. The diagonal of my desk is ✎ ruler lengths.
4. The perimeter of my desk is ✎ ruler lengths.
5. The width of my desk is ✎ ruler lengths.

You will need a one metre ruler to measure your classroom. Copy these sentences and work out the answers.
1. The length of my classroom is ✎ m.
2. The width of my classroom is ✎ m.
3. The diagonal of my classroom is ✎ m.
4. The width of the door is ✎ m.
5. The perimeter of my classroom is ✎ m.
6. The length of my desk is ✎ m.

Choose a partner to measure. You should measure in centimetres (cm). Choose your measuring equipment carefully. Here are some things you could use.

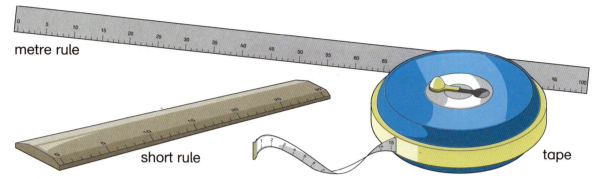

metre rule

short rule

tape

Take it in turns to measure each other and complete this table.

Name of person measured _____	Cm	Instrument used
1 Height		
2 Length of feet		
3 Length of arms		
4 Distance round head		
5 Distance from wrist to tip of middle finger		
6 Distance across shoulders		

Look carefully at each of the following. Would you measure them in metres (m) or centimetres (cm)?

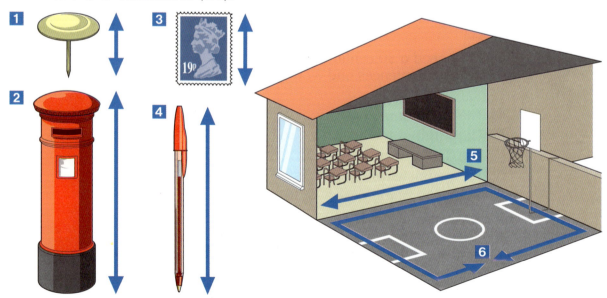

Now look back at your work in this lesson.
- Do you know the length of a metre and a centimetre?
- Do you know how to use metres and centimetres to estimate lengths of rooms or books?

❻ Mind skills with numbers

Most people like to go for a drink on a hot day. What is your favourite drink? What is the best way to buy a cola drink? Is it by the glass in a café, buying a can or buying a bottle? This is called 'best value for money'.

Write the answers to these questions.

1 If one glass of cola costs 50p, how much will four glasses cost?

2 If one packet of crisps costs 31p, how much will three packets cost?

3 If one cake costs 70p, how much will five cakes cost?

4 If one chocolate biscuit costs 33p, how much will three biscuits cost?

5 If one doughnut costs 22p, how much will four doughnuts cost?

6 If one bar of chocolate costs 32p, how much will three bars cost?

Write the answers to these questions.

1 20 - 11   **4** 9 + 11

2 19 - 6   **5** 8 + 12

3 30 - 4   **6** 14 + 6

Write six different ways of adding coins so that they total exactly 10p.

D

Pretend today's date is 28 December.
Copy these sentences and fill in the blanks.

1. Christmas Day was ✳ days ago.
2. New Year's Day will be in ✳ days.
3. If the first day of term is on 3 January, there are ✳ more days of holiday.
4. If the last day of term was 22 December, I have already had ✳ days of holiday.
5. Boxing Day was ✳ days ago.
6. Angie's birthday was exactly one week ago. The date of her birthday is ✳ December.

E

Sandra and her friends each have £20 to spend. For each question, write 'yes' if the girl has enough money and 'no' if she does not.

£13.00

£4.00

History of Fashion

£3.10

Life of a Dog

£4.00

Beat Route
number 34
Latest Releases
Interviews
Clubs
Dance

£2.20

Phantom of the Opera

£12.00

Pencils

£4.50

1. Sandra wants a pencil case, a single CD and a pen.
2. Helen wants two books and one CD album.
3. Rushna wants a school sweatshirt, a new pencil case and a single CD.
4. Jackie wants a CD album, a pencil case and a book.
5. Fatima wants two single CDs, two books and a magazine.
6. Amy wants a CD album, two magazines and a new pencil case.

F

Look around you in the classroom, through the window, or try to imagine things.

1. List three things that have a length of less than 20 cm.
2. List three things that have a length of between 20 cm and 10 m.
3. List three things that have a length of more than 10 m.

Now look back at your work in this lesson.
- Which exercises in this lesson did you like best?
- Which mathematical word in this lesson have you understood better than before?

Module B4

Shape and space

1 **Vertical symmetry**
Recognising a design which has a vertical line of symmetry and producing designs with at least one line of symmetry

2 **Half-way marks on scales**
Reading scales and dials to the marks that lie half-way between divisions numbered in ones or twos

3 **Half the number**
Finding ways to find the half of a whole number and to understand when to half and when to double a number

4 **Mid-point**
Estimating the mid-point of an edge and the centre of a surface

5 **Regular shapes**
Using and applying the skills related to line symmetry and halving in problem-solving. Gathering information into a table and using this to make and test predictions

6 **Symmetry and halving skills**
Using and applying skills in mid-way positions both in shape and in number in a mixed setting. Miscellaneous problems drawing on the earlier learning objectives

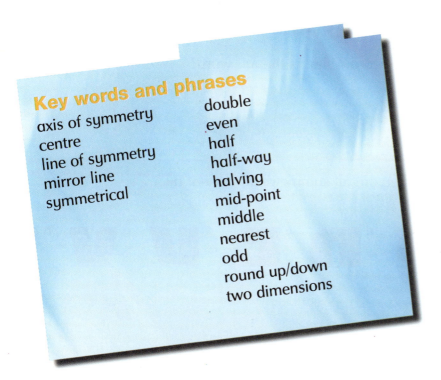

Key words and phrases

axis of symmetry
centre
line of symmetry
mirror line
symmetrical

double
even
half
half-way
halving
mid-point
middle
nearest
odd
round up/down
two dimensions

① Vertical symmetry

Can you see or think of other things that have a left–right symmetry?
What is 'symmetry', and why do we call this kind of symmetry vertical?

1 Use a mirror to decide which of these car logos has a line of symmetry.

2 This is half of a capital letter.

Trace it. Now fold the tracing paper on the dotted line and copy your tracing on the clean half of the tracing fold. Unfold the paper and you will see the full letter.

3 Use the same method as above to create your own shape with a line of symmetry.
4 Here is half a symmetrical word. What is the full word?

Look at these half letters. They are all symmetrical, but not all vertically symmetrical.

1 Use tracing paper to copy them.
2 Fold the paper on the dotted line and copy the half shape on the tracing paper.
3 Open the shape out and you will see the full letter.

C These words all have a line of symmetry but you have been given only half of the word. Use symmetry to work out what the full word should be.

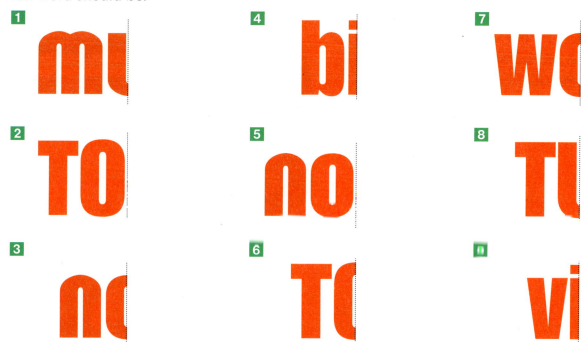

1	mu
4	bi
7	wc
2	TO
5	no
8	TU
3	nc
6	TC
9	vi

D These shapes have more than one line of symmetry. Trace them and use the tracing paper to help you find all the lines of symmetry.

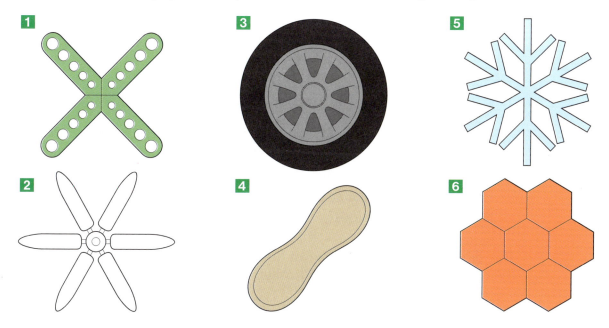

Now look back at your work in this lesson.
- Do you know when a shape has a vertical line of symmetry or not?
- Can you make a symmetrical shape?

② Half-way marks on scales

What are the two scores in this game? How can we tell when there is no number to read?

 These scales measures only whole or half pounds.

1 How many pounds of onions are there?
2 How many pounds of carrots?
3 How many of tomatoes?

This dial measures the number of turns that are made inside the car engine. These are called called 'revs' for short.

4 What revs are shown on these dials?

There are six snooker tables in this club. You pay for your game by putting money in the slot machine, and that gives you 30 minutes of light on your table. A timer shows how many minutes of light you have left.

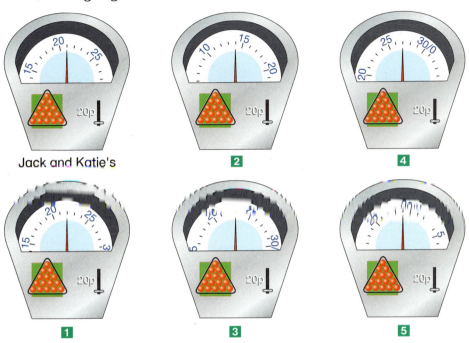

Jack and Katie's table has 21 minutes of light shown on their timer. How much time do the other snooker tables have?

The next evening Jack and Katie are waiting for a table. They work out that the timers will finish in the following order: table 2, table 5, table 1, table 3, table 4, table 6.

Say which table belongs to which timer.

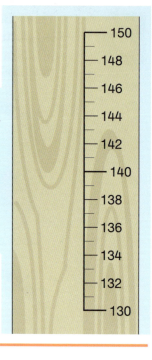

During the 'health week' in school all the pupils were measured. Roma and her friends made the following list of their heights, starting with the tallest. Josie was the tallest.

Name	Height	Name	Height
Angela	136 cm	Josie	140 cm
Roma	149 cm	Tracey	139 cm
Maria	142 cm	Jameela	135 cm

Copy this chart and mark the names with an arrow against their height.

Roll a pair of dice. Put the numbers you get on the dice together to make a two-digit number.

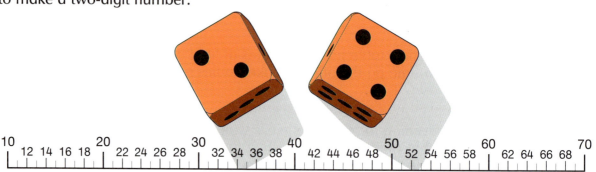

This could be 24 or 42. We want the largest number so we choose 42.

Copy the scale. Roll the dice and mark your two-digit number. Repeat this ten times.

1 What is the largest number which you marked on the scale?
2 What is the largest possible number which could be marked on the scale?
3 What is the smallest number which you marked on the scale?
4 What is the smallest possible number which could be marked on the scale?

Now look back at your work in this lesson.
• Can you read marks in scales or dials even if they do not have a number?
• Where do you still see scales and dials?

③ Half the number

This brother and sister are out trick or treating. They have promised to share the treats they collect equally.

1 A box of chocolates contains eight cream centres, twelve toffees and five nut centres. Share these chocolates equally between the two friends.

2 Use this recipe to make a large chocolate sticky cake.

Chocolate sticky cake

8 cups cornflakes
7 tablespoons golden syrup
7 tablespoons cocoa
1 cup icing sugar
small tub margarine

Work out what the quantities would be for two such cakes.

3 Each member of a class brings in the money they raised during charity week. The money is split equally between the school fund and the RSPCA. Here are the totals collected by five pupils. What are the five amounts which will be donated to the RSPCA?

Zoë	£18
Abbey	£9
Dominic	£16
Graham	£3
Michelle	£14

Ebony and Claire are sisters. They share a bedroom and have saved up to decorate it. They share the costs equally between them. Here are the costs.

Wallpaper border	£14
Paint for stencilling	£9
Stencils	£12
Waste bin	£3
Bean bag	£16
Lamp	£12

Write a list to show what Ebony's share of the total cost must be.

C Matthew takes his younger brother and sister out 'trick or treating' at Halloween. They collect toffees, lollipops, apples, boiled sweets, chewing gum and chocolate biscuits in one bag and share them out between the two younger children when they get home. Here is the whole collection of treats. How many of each should the children get?

D The local music store holds a half-price sale. Here are the prices before the sale. What will they be when they are at half-price?

Oasis album	£14
Spice Girls T-shirt	£8
Boyzone poster	£7
Aqua single	£4
Hanson double album	£18
Mixed sheet of pop stickers	£1

E Shake a pair of dice. Add the two numbers together and then halve the result.

$3 + 5 = 8$ Half of 8 is 4

1 Make a table for your results.

1st number	2nd number	Addition	Half
3	5	8	4

2 Do ten rolls and enter them on your table.
3 What is the smallest number you can get in the final column?
4 What is the largest number you can get in the final column?

Now look back at your work in this lesson.
- Do you know when to half and when to double a number?
- What is your way of finding half of 18?

④ Mid-point

Should the goalkeeper stand in the middle of the goal?
What are the advantages and the disadvantages?

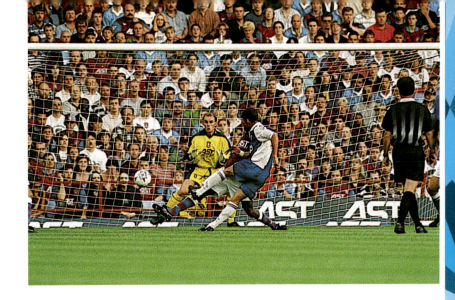

A

Trace this line on a tracing paper.

1 Without measuring, put a mark roughly on the centre of the line.

Check the accuracy of your centre by folding.

2 Is this mid-point accurately marked?

3 Trace this shape and place a point at its centre.

Check the accuracy of the centre by folding.

4 Is the centre accurately marked?

B

Trace these lines. Without measuring, put a mark roughly on the centre of each line.

Check the accuracy of your centre by folding.

C

Are these mid-points accurately marked?

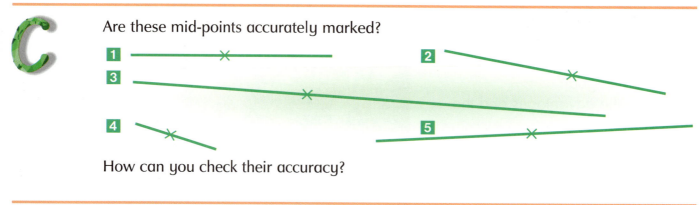

How can you check their accuracy?

D

Trace each of these shapes and place a point at their centre.

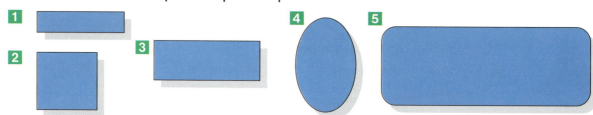

Check the accuracy of the centre by folding.

E

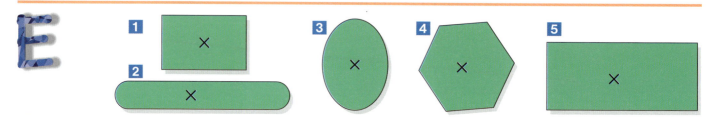

Look at these shapes. Which of these centres are accurately marked?

F

You will need an entire page for this exercise.

1 Draw a set of goal posts in the middle at the top of your page.
2 Draw a small matchstick man in the middle of the left side of your page.
3 Draw a circle in the centre of the page.
4 Draw a small matchstick man half-way along the bottom of the page.
5 Draw a pair of goal posts half-way down the right-hand side of the page.
6 Check your final pictures by imagining the two men shooting at the goals opposite them. They should be perfectly lined up. Now imagine them walking straight across or straight up the page. They should meet in the circle in the centre.

> Now look back at your work in this lesson.
> • Do you know how to find the half-way mark of a line?
> • What about the mid-point of a table or a desk?

⑤ Regular shapes

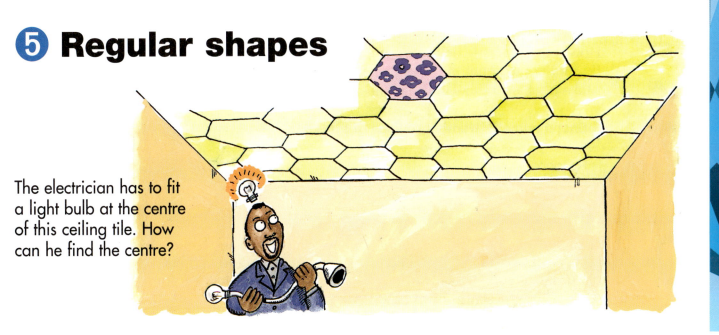

The electrician has to fit a light bulb at the centre of this ceiling tile. How can he find the centre?

Each of the shapes shown here is regular which means they have sides of equal lengths. Trace each shape. Now decide which of these methods will locate the exact centre.

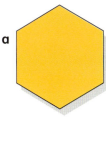
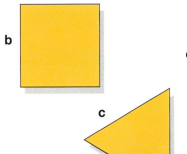
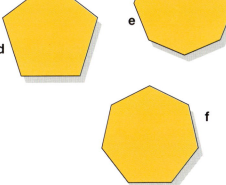

a   b   c   d   e   f

Method one
Join each corner to the opposite corner (that makes a diagonal). The centre is where the diagonals cross.

Method two
Mark the half-way point on one side and join that mark to the opposite corner. The centre is where all these lines meet.

Find out the names of each of the shapes in exercise A. Now find their exact centres by using one of the methods given.
Make a table to show which shapes needed method 1 and which needed method 2. Count the number of triangles that the shape is split into by the lines you have drawn. Include this number in the third column of your table. The first one is done for you.

Shape name	Method	Number of triangles
Hexagon	2	6

C How many lines of symmetry do the shapes in exercise A have?
Be sure not to count the lines twice.
Make a table to show your findings. The first one is done for you.

Shape name	Number of lines of symmetry
Hexagon	6

D Look back at all the information you have gathered. You should
be able to make some predictions about what you could find out
about a nine- and ten-sided regular polygon. Ask your teacher for a
copy of these shapes to test your prediction.

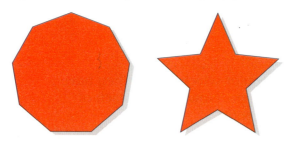

E For each of these dog shapes write down the name of the
polygon it is made of and whether the shape is regular or not
regular. The first one is done for you.

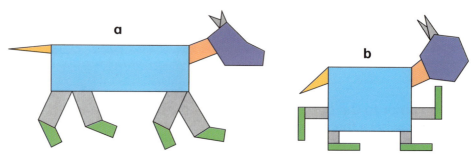

Part of body	Shape	Dog A	Dog B
Head	hexagon	not regular	regular
Body			
Tail			
Ears			
Foot	quadrilateral		

Now look back at your work in this lesson.
- Can you collect information in a table?
- Can you use the table to guess something?

⑥ Symmetry and halving skills

How many lines of symmetry
do you think you have?

Answer the following questions.

1 This kite has a single line of symmetry. Find its other half.

a   b   c

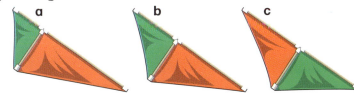

2 How much longer has this
cake to cook if the oven
timer shows the time still
needed?

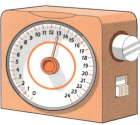

3 Duncan sells his tennis racket for half of the price he paid.
If he paid £20 what will he sell for?

4 Trace and mark the mid-point of these lines.

a

b

Each of these aliens has a single line of symmetry.

1 Make a list of the halves that match.
2 Which aliens are missing their other half?

C As part of a check on lateness to school in the morning the Deputy Headteacher checks the time of all late arrivals. Here is the table she made with the times missing.

Below are the readings on her stopwatch. She wrote the students' names down as they arrived at school. Fill in the correct times.

Name	Time
Nadia	
Michael	
Fiona	
Blanquis	
Paul	

D The local sports shop holds a half-price sale. Here are the prices before the sale. What will they be when they are at half-price?

1 T-shirt £16
2 Set of sweat bands £9
3 Tracksuit bottoms £14
4 Running vest £12
5 Tube of tennis balls £7
6 Leeds United football shirt £18

E Copy the square.

1 Mark the mid-point of each side of this square and join the mid-points. What shape do you get?
2 Repeat this until the drawing is too small to do.
3 Draw your own oblong and see if the same type of pattern appears.
4 Draw another shape and try the same thing again.

Now look back at your work in this lesson.
• Which is easier for you to do: find the mid-point of a line or the line of symmetry of a shape?
• Which mathematical words in this lesson do you understand better than before?

Practise your skills

Number and money

Write these amounts in words.

1 £8.82
2 £7.06
3 £2.60

This is how £2.60 looks on a calculator.

Write these amounts in figures.

4 Three pounds and eight pence
5 Six pounds and sixty pence

Handling data

Claire is 170 cm,
Nishi is 159 cm,
Rakhee is 165 cm,
Amanda is 168 cm and
Susan is 164 cm tall.

Can you give a name to each of the girls in the picture?

Number and algebra

Look carefully at each of the following. Then write whether you would measure them in metres (m) or centimetres (cm).

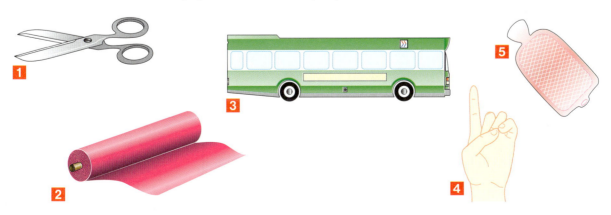

Shape and space

Write down whether each of these shapes has a line of symmetry or not.
Remember that everything on either side of a line of symmetry must be the same.

1
2
3
4
5
6

Now try this...

Imagine that you can choose one thing from each box.
List all the different pairs of things you can choose.

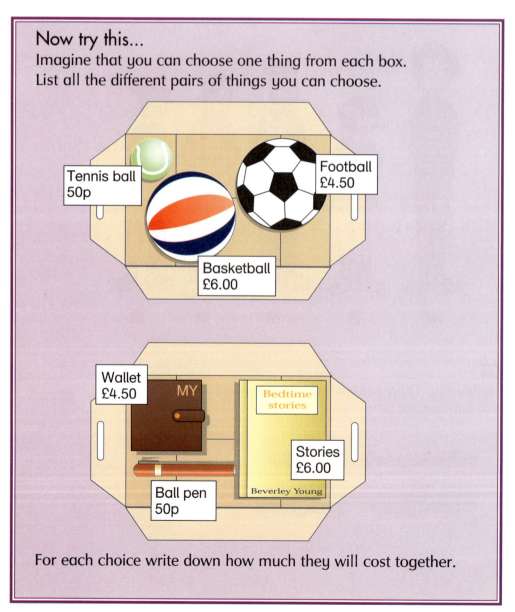

Tennis ball
50p

Football
£4.50

Basketball
£6.00

Wallet
£4.50

MY

Bedtime
stories

Stories
£6.00

Beverley Young

Ball pen
50p

For each choice write down how much they will cost together.

Check your skills

You can check how well you can do the things listed here. Get your parents and friends to help check them. Your teacher will give you a copy of this page to tick on.

Number and money

1 I can read and write amounts of money in figures and words. ☐
2 I know when there is enough money to pay for something. ☐
3 I can choose from a collection of coins and notes (or stamps and vouchers) to make up a sum. I know when the exact amount is not possible to make up, and how best to deal with that. ☐
4 I can give change for any amount from a £1 or a £2 coin. I can find ways of making up the change if the right coins are not all there. ☐
5 I know roughly how much things cost, and that the prices in different shops may be different but within a range. ☐

Handling data

1 I can record information about things in an organised way, e.g. in lists. ☐
2 I know my own sizes such shoes and clothes and also personal facts such as my full name and address and date of birth. ☐
3 I can say which containers of the same make are bigger or smaller than others by looking not only at the height. ☐
4 I can find ways to know which of two containers holds more. ☐
5 I know what things are measured in millilitres (or cubic centimetres), litres and cubic metres. ☐

Numbers in the mind

1 I know when to add or take away numbers, and can do that without pen and paper or calculator when the numbers are small. ☐
2 I can keep track of numbers when adding a number more than once, or when taking away numbers more than once. ☐
3 I can describe in words a method of adding or taking away numbers in my head. ☐
4 When something is much bigger than the unit of measure then I know how to repeat measure and keep track of the total. ☐
5 I know how long a metre and a centimetre are, and can use these to estimate lengths. ☐

Shape and space

1 I know when a design has a vertical line of symmetry and can complete or produce designs with a line of symmetry. ☐
2 I can read scales and dials to the marks that lie half-way between divisions numbered in ones or twos. ☐
3 I can find half of a whole number such as 9 and 16 and understand when to half and when to double a number. ☐
4 I can roughly find the centre of a table and the mid-point of an edge. ☐
5 I can use the skills on symmetry and halving to find the mid-point of regular shapes. ☐

Module **B**5

Number and algebra

1 **Just add the ten**

Knowing how to add numbers such as 30 + 40 together, and how to add 10 to numbers, or take away 10 from numbers, without pencil and paper or calculator

2 **Adding in your head**

Working out in the head how to add numbers such as 20, 50 or 60 to or from numbers such as 14 and 36. Using this skill in solving word problems

3 **A thousand, more or less**

Knowing which of two three-digit numbers is bigger and where a thousand comes in the number sequence

4 **Counting in 2s, 5s and 10s**

Counting in 2s, 5s, and 10s forward and back

5 **Doing the opposite**

Knowing what to do to go back from a position of a number, by doing the opposite action to what has been done before

6 **Large number skills**

Revising and practising the skills learned in this module

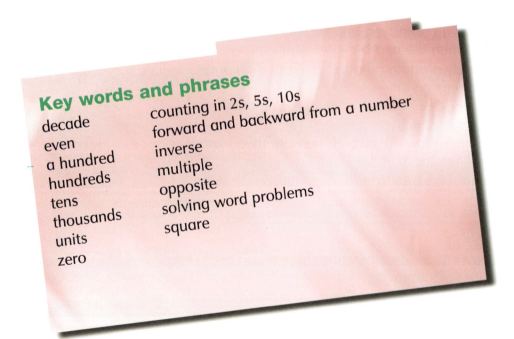

Key words and phrases

decade
even
a hundred
hundreds
tens
thousands
units
zero

counting in 2s, 5s, 10s
forward and backward from a number
inverse
multiple
opposite
solving word problems
square

① Just add the ten

"At the third stroke the time will be eight, thirty-seven and ten seconds...."

This is the Sultan Abdul Samad Building in Kuala Lumpur.
Do you know any other famous clocks?
Have you ever seen Big Ben?

You can find out the exact time by phoning 123 on most phones. The precise time is announced every ten seconds.
The following times have just been announced.
For each one, give the next two times.
1 6:05 and 10 seconds
2 8:15 and 20 seconds
3 12:02 and 30 seconds
4 14:25 and 10 seconds
5 15:31 and 50 seconds
6 17:48 and 30 seconds

Write the answers to these questions.
1 $36 + 10 = $ ✳
2 $87 + 10 = $ ✳
3 $45 + 10 = $ ✳
4 $14 + 10 = $ ✳
5 $66 + 10 = $ ✳
6 $73 + 10 = $ ✳

Answer the following questions.

1 Roger's uncle drives a taxi. The price shown on his meter increases in 10p jumps. Copy this table and write in the prices that will show on his meter.

		1st Jump	2nd Jump	3rd Jump
a	£2.40	→ ❀	→ ❀	→ ❀
b	£3.10	→ ❀	→ ❀	→ ❀
c	£1.50	→ ❀	→ ❀	→ ❀
d	£4.20	→ ❀	→ ❀	→ ❀

2 Rushna's class are doing a sponsored silence to raise money. For the first five minutes they earn 15p. For each five minutes after this, they earn 10p. Here are their sponsored silence times.

Rushna	15 minutes
Harry	10 minutes
Josie	25 minutes
Wasim	20 minutes
Curtley	35 minutes

Copy the table and then fill it in to show how much each of them earns. Rushna's earnings have been done for you.

	Time (min.)	5	10	15	20	25	30	35	40
	Rushna	15		35					
a	Harry	15	❀						
b	Josie	15				❀			
c	Wasim	15			❀				
d	Curtley	15						❀	

A new record shop is giving away record vouchers to some flats in the buildings on Vicky's estate. These have been written in the table. The first flat is chosen in a lucky draw. Then a voucher is given to every 10th flat.

		1st Flat	2nd Flat	3rd Flat
1	Crocus House	17		
2	Primrose House	48		
3	Rose House	32		
4	Tulip House	4		
5	Daffodil House	61		
6	Sunflower House	23		

Copy the table and then fill in the numbers of the lucky flats.

Now look back at your work in this lesson.
- Do you know how to add numbers such as 30 + 40 together in your head?
- Do you know how to add 10 to numbers, or take away 10 from numbers in your head?

❷ Adding in your head

Here is a picture of the Bee Gees at the Brit Awards of 1997. This is 30 years after their first hit! Can you work out in your head which year that was? Do you know of any other artists who have been popular for so long? Which of the present groups do you think will be popular in 30 years' time?

Work these out in your head

1 56 + 20		**4** 50 + 38	
2 30 + 43		**5** 26 + 60	
3 45 + 40		**6** 18 + 80	

Rachel's class agrees to give 20p each towards a collection for a dog for a blind person. After they have donated 20p, how much will each person have left?

		Money in pocket or purse	Amount after donation
1	Rachel	62p	✳
2	Debbie	75p	✳
3	Harshad	66p	✳
4	Winston	84p	✳
5	Linda	77p	✳
6	Pete	£1.10p	✳

Copy the table and fill in the amounts left without using a calculator.

Mobab and his friends have Saturday jobs. They each get a pay rise of 30p per hour. Copy the table and fill in either the new or the old rates of pay.

		Old rate	Rate after 30p rise
1	Mobab	£3.30	?
2	Kelly	?	£4.70
3	Shariff	£3.40	?
4	Mandy	?	£2.90
5	Fatima	£3.70	?
6	Bill	?	£3.35

D

Paul and his friends watch their local football team. They read in the programme that all prices will be increased by 30p from the next home game.

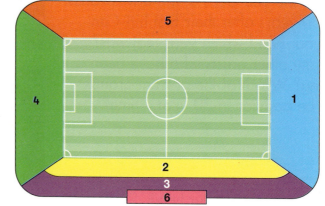

1 South stand £6.20
2 Enclosure £7.00
3 West stand £9.70
4 North stand £10.50
5 East stand £11.30
6 Luxury box £72.20

1 Write what the new prices are.

2 Paul and four friends have £55 in total. They want to sit together. What are the best seats they can afford?

E

You will need a calculator. Use the 'repeat add' idea to keep adding the same number with one stroke. Find out how your calculator does that. For example, to increase the number 4 by 2 each time you may have to press: `4 + 2 = =`

Or you may have to press: `4 + + 2 =`

After that each time you press `=` the number is increased by 2.

In the following examples, enter the number shown, then press:
`+ 1 0 = =`   Write down the next three answers for each of these questions. The first one is done for you.

1 7 → 17 → 27 → 37   **4** 66 →
2 16 →   **5** 53 →
3 48 →   **6** 27 →

F

Without using a calculator, write down the next three answers.
1 Add 10.   8 →   **4** Subtract 10.   95 →
2 Add 10.   18 →   **5** Subtract 10.   65 →
3 Add 10.   87 →   **6** Subtract 10.   77 →

Now look back at your work in this lesson.
- Can you work out in your head how to add numbers such as 20, 50 or 60 to or from numbers such as 14 and 36?
- Do you find your method easier than working this out on paper?

③ A thousand, more or less

This is a picture of the Dome that celebrates the second Millennium in the year 2000. What would you put in the Dome? Will you visit the Dome? There would probably have been celebrations at the first Millennium. Can you imagine these?

Put these dates from the first Millennium in the correct order. Then say how many years it is from the last one until the year 1000. The first one is done for you.

1 768, 802, 536, 425, 760, 800
   425, 536, 760, 768, 800, 802 – 198 years until 1000.

2 450, 399, 401, 375, 480, 370

3 620, 618, 545, 600, 519, 505

4 818, 828, 808, 804, 714, 799

5 362, 348, 375, 350, 363, 301

6 929, 919, 892, 896, 915, 900

Wayne and his friends belong to a snooker club. They have all been ranked in the top 1000 British players. Look at the rankings and then answer the questions.

1 Who is the highest ranking player?
2 Who is the lowest ranking player?
3 Who is ranked second?
4 Who is ranked third?
5 Who is ranked fourth?
6 Who is ranked fifth?

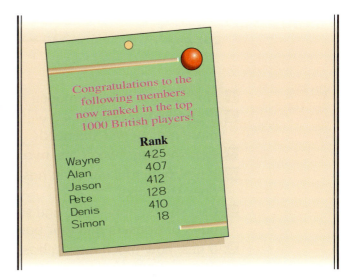

Congratulations to the following members now ranked in the top 1000 British players!

	Rank
Wayne	425
Alan	407
Jason	412
Pete	128
Denis	410
Simon	18

Rutinder's uncle gives her a surprise present of £1000 to spend on clothes. She can't decide what to buy. Help her to work out some of the possibilities. Work with a partner and use a calculator.

Raincoat £120
Trousers £63
Shoes £64

Coat £160
Skirt £42
Shoes £64

£85
£170
£120
£43
£42
£160
£31
£64

1 Has she got enough money to buy one of every item?

2 If yes, how much money will she have left? If no, how much more money will she need?

3 Can she buy: two coats, two suits and two pairs of trousers?

4 If yes, how much money has she left? If no, how much more does she need?

5 Can she buy one coat, one suit, one raincoat, four skirts, four pairs of trousers and four pairs of shoes?

6 If yes, how much money has she left? If no, how much more does she need?

Gary enjoys reading long books! The book he is reading has 1000 pages. Work out how many pages he has left to read each day.

	Pages read	Pages left
Monday	25	975
Tuesday	32	
Wednesday	17	
Thursday	21	
Friday	10	
Saturday	42	
Sunday	31	

Copy and complete the table. Monday has been done for you.

Roger and Anna are doing work experience in an office. They have to file some papers.

Which drawer should the papers go in?
1 1003
2 702
3 1031
4 425
5 452
6 786

Now look back at your work in this lesson.
• Do you know which number is bigger: 412 or 389?
• Can you count from 1003 backwards to 990?

④ Counting in 2s, 5s and 10s

New coin designs are brought out all the time. Which of these coins and notes have you ever used?

A

Ruth's aunt pays for everything at the shops with a £5 note. She keeps getting lots of change! She keeps the £2, £1, 50p and 20p coins but gives the 1p, 2p, 5p and 10p coins to Ruth. Work out how much she gives Ruth each day.

1 Sunday

2 Monday

3 Tuesday

4 Wednesday

5 Thursday

6 Friday

B

Andrew and his friends like music. They each have a different favourite single. The table shows how the songs moved in the charts during a month. Copy the table and fill in the boxes.

	1st week		2nd week		3rd week		4th week
1 Andrew	28	+2	✳	+10	✳	-5	✳
2 Shripa	56	+10	✳	+10	✳	+10	✳
3 Bobby	8	-2	✳	-5	✳	+2	✳
4 Curtley	48	+10	✳	+5	✳	+10	✳
5 Rushna	35	+5	✳	+5	✳	+5	✳
6 Liz	12	-2	✳	-5	✳	-5	✳

7 Whose favourite single finished highest at the end of the month?

C

Write the missing numbers.

1 6, ✳, 10, 12, 14, ✳
2 5, 10, ✳, 20, ✳, 30
3 24, 34, 44, ✳, ✳, 74

4 7, 12, ✳, 22, ✳, 32
5 17, ✳, 21, 23, 25, ✳
6 86, ✳, 66, 56, ✳, 36

D

Three different bus companies go to the station:
Red Buses run every two minutes,
Blue Buses run every five minutes
and Green Buses run every ten minutes.
All three companies have buses which leave the station on the
hour every hour, for example 8 o'clock, 9 o'clock, and so on.

1 In the first 20 minutes a Red Bus will arrive on ten occasions.
Write down the minutes past the hour of each arrival.

2 In the first 20 minutes a Blue Bus will arrive on four occasions.
Write down the minutes past the hour of each arrival.

3 In the first 20 minutes a Green Bus will arrive on two occasions.
Write down the minutes past the hour of each arrival.

4 Are there any times when all three buses will arrive at the
station at the same time (apart from on the hour)?

5 Are there any times when only two buses will arrive at the
station at the same time? What do you think is the reason
for that?

E

The three bus companies had all charged the same fares but
now they are being changed as follows:
Red Bus up 5p
Blue Bus up 2p
Green Bus down 2p
Copy the table and fill in the new fares.

	Old price	Red Bus +5p	Blue Bus +2p	Green Bus -2p
1 To shops	30p			
2 To school	35p			
3 To church	40p			
4 To library	50p			
5 To park	55p			
6 To next village	70p			

Now look back at your work in this lesson.
- Can you count backwards in 2s from 50 to 30? And in 5s from 30 to 50?
- How far can you count in 10s starting from 10?

⑤ Doing the opposite

This is the world's tallest building – the Petronas Towers in Kuala Lumpur. It is 88 storeys high. What is the opposite of saying 'going up 88 floors'?

Think about the opposites of these words, then copy the sentences and write in the opposite word.
The opposite of:

1 Buying a CD is _____ a CD.
2 Running forwards is running _____.
3 Going up in a lift is going _____ in a lift
4 Going in to a shop is coming _____ of a shop
5 Opening a book is _____ a book
6 Turning left is turning _____.

Rewrite these questions as division sums. The first one is done for you.

1 7 x 2 = 14   14 ÷ 2 =   4 10 x 5 = 50
2 8 x 3 = 24   5 6 x 11 = 66
3 9 x 4 = 36   6 6 x 6 = 36

Rushna and her sisters are each given £50 by their uncle. Each of them opens a savings account and promises not to let their balance go below £50.

Each time they earn money, they pay it in. They can withdraw it at a later date.

Write in their balances to check if they have kept their promise.

1 Rushna's balance is £53. She pays in £10. Later she withdraws £20. What is her new balance?
2 Shripa's balance is £50. She pays in £25. Later she withdraws £50. What is her new balance?
3 Fatima's balance is £50. She pays in £5. Later she withdraws £10. What is her new balance?
4 Nazmin's balance is £50. She pays in £50. Later she withdraws £10. What is her new balance?
5 Rutinder's balance is £50. She pays in £33. Later she withdraws £30. What is her new balance?
6 Fahema's balance is £50. She pays in £35. Later she withdraws £45. What is her new balance?

D

Andrew was watching his cable television. He thinks he knows all the channels and can move from one to the other with closed eyes.

Follow his moves on his cable box display and write down the channels that he will obtain in each question. In each row only one number is written but the two moves should help you find the other two numbers.

CH20

1	Ch 20	Forward 5	→	Ch ☐	Back 5	→	Ch ☐
2	Ch 32	Forward 8	→	Ch ☐	Back 8	→	Ch ☐
3	Ch ☐	Forward 10	→	Ch 11	Back 10	→	Ch ☐
4	Ch ☐	Forward 6	→	Ch 26	Back 6	→	Ch ☐
5	Ch ☐	Forward 7	→	Ch ☐	Back 7	→	Ch 41
6	Ch ☐	Forward 12	→	Ch ☐	Back 12	→	Ch 14

E

Kevin's uncle has an ice-cream van. Look at his prices.

ice lolly 42p

'99' 78p

ice-cream tub 55p

cornet 52p

ice-cream lolly 67p

choc ice 64p

Chilly Miller Ice Creams

He puts his prices up by 20p on every item. Write the new price of each item.

1 Choc ice
2 Cornet
3 '99'
4 Ice lolly
5 Ice-cream lolly
6 Ice-cream tub

He loses customers, so he decides to reduce his prices by 10p on every item. Fill in his new prices.

7 Choc ice
8 Cornet
9 '99'p
10 Ice lolly
11 Ice-cream lolly
12 Ice-cream tub

5 Number and algebra

Sarah's class are on a week's school journey and they stay at a hostel.

The driver must travel no more than 90 miles in the day. The journey recorder in the bus is turned back to 0 when they arrive at the hostel.

Sarah keeps a diary of how many miles they travel each day, because the driver is paid by the total miles. She writes the number of miles travelled each time, and the total up to then.

For example:

Monday   Went to theme park

1 Travelled 42 miles.   She writes 'travelled 42' then 'total 42'.

2 Travelled back to hostel.   She writes 'travelled 42' then 'total 84'.

Show what numbers she will write down in each of these trips for the journey and the total.

Tuesday   Went to swimming baths

3 Travelled 25 miles.

4 Travelled back to hostel.

Wednesday   Went to Sealife Centre

5 Travelled 58 miles.

6 Travelled back to hostel.

Thursday   Went to museum

7 Travelled 8 miles.

8 Travelled back to hostel.

Friday   Went to wildlife park

9 Travelled 10 miles.

10 Travelled back to hostel.

Now look back at your work in this lesson.

- Do you know what is the opposite of climbing up the seven steps? Do you know the opposite of turning to the left?

- If you start from a number and add 10 you get 35. What number did you start with?

⑥ Large number skills

Which airport could this be? Have you ever travelled
on an aircraft? Which countries have you visited?
When aircraft leave an airport, they 'take off'.
What is the inverse, or opposite, of 'take off'?

Think about the inverse or opposite of the
following actions.
The opposite of:

1 Adding a number is _____ a number

2 Multiplying a number is _____ a number

3 Turning up the heat is _____ _____
   the heat

4 Igniting a fire is _____ _____ a fire

5 Accelerating your speed is _____ your
   speed

6 Dressing in the morning is _____ at
   bedtime.

Write the answers to these questions.

1 18 + 10 =   **4** 18 + 5 + 5 =

2 76 - 10 =   **5** 95 - 10 - 5 - 2 =

3 25 + 2 + 2 + 2 =   **6** 73 - 10 - 2 - 2 - 2 =

Shop A and Shop B are in competition. They charge exactly the
same price for every item. Then Shop A increases its prices by 5p
and Shop B increases its prices by 10p. Copy this table and fill
in the new prices.

		Old price	Shop A New price	Shop B New price
1	Crisps	34p		
2	Cola drink	42p		
3	Nuts	36p		
4	Chocolate bar	52p		
5	Bag of sweets	86p		
6	Cream egg	32p		

John and Helen work in the office of their local football club.
Help them put these membership cards in order.

1 Membership card — Membership number 686 — Name: Thomas Morgan — 668, 670, 598, 702, 687

4 Membership card — Membership number 786 — Name: William Becket — 792, 754, 708, 780, 756

2 Membership card — Membership number 485 — Name: Gladys Tilbury — 480, 489, 426, 451, 409

5 Membership card — Membership number 128 — Name: Frederick Macintosh — 126, 124, 117, 139, 125

3 Membership card — Membership number 323 — Name: Joe Bloggs — 333, 298, 321, 356, 308

6 Membership card — Membership number 989 — Name: Samantha Louise — 999, 987, 890, 962, 998

Debbie has borrowed £100 from her mum. Each week she pays
some of it back. Work out how much she pays back each month.

		Week 1	Week 2	Week 3	Week 4	Total for month
1	Jan	£5	0	£2	£10	
2	Feb	£10	£2	£2	£2	
3	Mar	£5	£2	0	£2	
4	Apr	£5	£5	£2	£2	
5	May	£2	£10	£10	£2	

6 How much has she paid back by the end of May?

How much does she still owe?

The first of these questions has been done for you. Copy the
questions into your book and then fill in the blanks.

#	op	start						
1	+10	6	→	16	→	26	→	36
2	-10	85	→	☼	→	☼	→	☼
3	+2	71	→	☼	→	☼	→	☼
4	-2	86	→	☼	→	☼	→	☼
5	+5	16	→	☼	→	☼	→	☼
6	-5	48	→	☼	→	☼	→	☼

Now look back at your work in this lesson.
- Are you more confident about adding numbers like 30 or 40 in your head?
- Have you learned how to work with large numbers and how to do inverse operations?

Module B6

Handling data

❶ Tables of data

Reading tables with numbers to answer questions from the information in the table. Summarising information from a survey into tables

❷ The middle size

Knowing roughly what the average length or the average height means, either by looking at a 'middle' or by finding a most common length or height

❸ One set diagram

Sorting things by what they have in common. Being able to show this by a diagram or in two lists

❹ Rows and columns

Understanding a table where the information is organised in rows and columns

❺ Certain, impossible and uncertain

Understanding when things are certain to happen or are impossible and that we cannot be sure about many other things

❻ Data skills

Revising the topics covered in this module

Key words and phrases

average
certain
impossible
in common
least popular
middle
most common
most popular
typical
uncertain
unlikely

columns
rows
set
set diagram
table
tally
total
two-way table

compare
order
sort

① Tables of data

Some lists have numbers that you can change, such as prices. Others cannot be changed, such as counts or totals. Can you tell in these two pictures which is which?

Damien asked all the pupils in his class what kind of home they lived in. Here is the table he made for his results.

Type of home	Number of pupils
Detached house	4
Semi-detached	8
Terrace	10
Flat	6
Bungalow	2

1 Where did the numbers in the table come from?
2 How many pupils live in a detached house?
3 How many live in a bungalow?
4 Do more pupils live in a semi-detached house or a flat?
5 Which kind of home is the most common?
6 Which was the least common?
7 Can you think of another kind of property which none of the pupils lived in?

Sasha kept a record of the match results of her local hockey team. This is her list for the first four months of the year.

1 Make a tally table of Sasha's results.
2 How many times did her team lose?
3 Were there more draws or more wins?
4 Do you think Sasha was pleased with her team?
5 Give a reason for Sasha's opinion.

Sally went out to with her family to a café. Here is the dessert menu.

Dessert menu	
Desserts	**Cost**
Choc. gateau	£1.25
Pavlova	£1.50
Cheesecake	£1.30
Apple pie	£1.00
Ice-cream	80p
Mousse	75p
Strawberries	£1.70

1 Sally chose the chocolate gateau. How much did it cost?
2 Sally's mum chose a pudding that cost £1.30. What did Sally's mum have?
3 Sally's dad wanted apple pie and ice-cream. Could he have this for under £2.00?
4 Both Sally's brothers had mousse. How much did that cost?
5 Was the cost for the two boys more or less than dad's sweet?
6 Who decides the prices in the menu?

Daniel did a survey to find out which colour his friends would prefer for a new school sweatshirt. He asked them to tick their choice on his list. Here is the result.

Colour	Tally	Total
Navy blue	✓✓✓✓✓✓✓	
Royal blue	✓✓✓	
Light blue	✓✓	
Green	✓✓✓✓	
Brown	✓✓✓✓	
Red	✓✓✓✓✓✓	
Mauve	✓✓✓✓✓	

1 Add up the ticks for each colour and make your own frequency table with the totals.
2 Which was the most popular colour?
3 Which two colours scored the same number of votes?
4 Which colour was the least popular choice?
5 How many friends did Daniel ask?
6 What does each tick in the table mean?
7 What do the numbers mean?

On Sports Day Year 8 was divided into four teams: the red team, the yellow team, the green team and the blue team. This table shows how many boys and girls were in each team.

Team	Girls	Boys
Blue	10	11
Green	9	12
Red	12	9
Yellow	13	8

1 How many girls were in the red team?
2 How many boys were in the blue team?
3 Which team had the most girls in it?
4 Which team had three more boys than girls?
5 How many pupils were in each team?
6 How many pupils in Year 9 took part in Sports Day?

Now look back at your work in this lesson.
• Can you answer questions from reading a table with numbers, knowing what the numbers are for?
• Can you make a table with numbers that are totals of things you have collected?

② The middle size

Could you use all of these hammers to knock a nail into a wall? Why not?

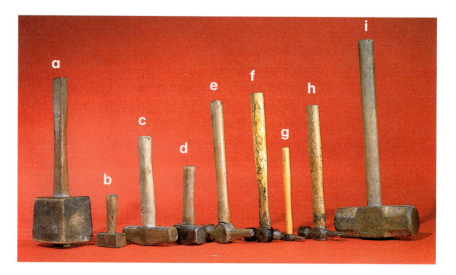

 Answer the following questions.
1. Which hammer would you say is of an average size?
2. How many of the hammers are larger than the one you chose?
3. How many of the hammers are smaller?
4. Do you still agree that the hammer you chose is the average size?

 Gemma is going riding. She needs an average size pony because she is too tall to ride a small one and not strong enough to manage the larger ones.

1. Which ponies would be too big for Gemma to handle?
2. Why would Gemma find it difficult to ride pony **d**?
3. Which would be the best pony for Gemma?

 An average size class in Petra's school has 28 pupils.
1. There are 42 pupils in class 5. Is this class larger or smaller than average?
2. Miss Evans has a smaller than average class. Can you suggest the number of pupils that might be in her class?
3. Class 7 is an average size class. There are the same number of boys and girls in this class. How many of each are there?

Last Saturday the local shoe shop sold lots of pairs of trainers. It sold three pairs of size 4, eight pairs of size 5, four pairs of size 6, 12 pairs of size 7, nine pairs of size 8 and four pairs of size 9 .

1 Which was the most popular size that they sold?

2 How many more of size 8 did they sell than size 9?

3 How many pairs of size 7 and size 8 did they sell altogether?

4 When the shop reorders trainers to stock the shelves, which three sizes would you expect them to order the most of?

The local primary school needs a new school bus.
Here are the buses they have looked at.

1 If they wanted a large bus which one should they choose?

2 If they decided that a small bus would be suitable which three should they choose from?

3 The headteacher decides that the two largest buses are too big. Which is the largest bus he would consider?

4 In the end everyone chooses the average size bus. Which one do you think that is?

5 What reason can you give for your answer?

Now look back at your work in this lesson.

- Can you choose an average size book in a pile of many books of different sizes?
- Did you make your decision by looking at the most common size or by choosing the middle size between the biggest and the smallest books?

③ One set diagram

If you sorted the people into two sets, how would you describe each set?

All the pupils from class C are invited to a party. Everyone wants to go but some are playing in a hockey match for the school. The diagram shows which of them are in the hockey team.

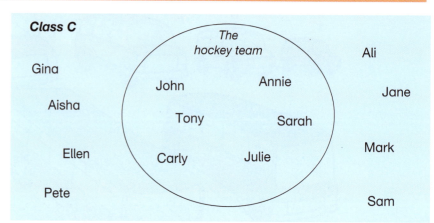

Class C

Gina
Aisha
Ellen
Pete

The hockey team
John   Annie
Tony   Sarah
Carly   Julie

Ali
Jane
Mark
Sam

1. Which pupils will not be able to accept the invitation?
2. How many of the group do not play hockey?
3. Name two girls going to the party.
4. What do you notice about all the team members?
5. If George, who is not in class C, receives an invitation as well do you think he would be able to go?

Here is a list of pets that are kept by Jameela's friends.

| cat | dog | rabbit | goldfish | gerbil | tortoise |
| hamster | snake | budgerigar | | | |

1. Draw one ring around all the animals that have fur. This is called a 'one set' diagram.
2. Which animals will be good pets for children that are allergic to animal fur?
3. Are there more furry animals or more without fur in Jameela's friends' pets?
4. If you were choosing a pet what would it be? Would it be inside or outside the set of furry animals?

C The Snack Bar has three different menus.

1. How many different hot drinks are available?
2. If you do not want anything hot, what drink could you choose?
3. Are there more hot or more cold drinks on the menu?
4. If you wanted to call the first menu 'the _____ menu' what would you choose for the missing word?
5. If you wanted to call the second menu 'the _____ menu' what would you choose for the missing word?
6. If you wanted to call the third menu 'the _____ menu' what would you choose for the missing word?

John and his friend go to the snack bar for lunch.

1. John chooses spaghetti bolognaise and his friend chooses a different hot snack. What could his friend have chosen?
2. Sabera buys beans on toast for her lunch on Monday. On Tuesday she wants a cold snack without bread. What would she choose?
3. Which hot snack would you buy?
4. Andrew wants a cold pudding. What could he have?
5. Molly wants a hot pudding but hates rice. What could she eat?
6. How many cold puddings are available?

Look again at the three menus in the Snack Bar.

1. Choose a meal that includes a hot snack, a cold pudding and a hot drink.
2. Now choose a different meal that has a cold snack, a hot pudding and a cold drink.
3. If all the hot food is sold out, find a snack, a pudding and a drink from the items that are left.

Now look back at your work in this lesson.
- Can you sort things by what they have in common?
- Can you show your sorting by a diagram or in two lists?

④ Rows and columns

Sometimes tables are very complicated. But there is one thing in common in all of them.
You must find the right column to read down and the right row to read across.

This two-way table shows the number of birthdays in January and February in Peter's class.

Birthdays	Boys	Girls
January	4	3
February	6	5

1 How many boys have their birthdays in January?
2 How many girls have their birthdays in February?
3 In which month do six boys have their birthdays?
4 How many birthdays are there altogether in January?
5 How many girls in Peter's class have their birthdays in the first two months of the year?

Lots of people want to buy these 'bargain' T-shirts! Look at the prices!

T-shirts	Women's	Men's
Small	£4.00	£4.50
Medium	£5.00	£5.50
Large	£6.00	£6.50

1 What is the cost of a small woman's T-shirt?
2 Mr Patel is a large man. How much would he pay for a new T-shirt?
3 Mrs Lee pays £5 for a T-shirt for herself. What size does she take?
4 She also buys a another one at £6 to give as a present. Do you think it is for a larger or smaller woman than herself?
5 Two identical T-shirts cost £11. What size are they and who are they for?
6 Mike buys two T-shirts, one for his mum and one for his dad. The total cost is £9.50. What sizes could his parents be?

C

Here is a two-way table showing the special names given to the family members of five different animals.

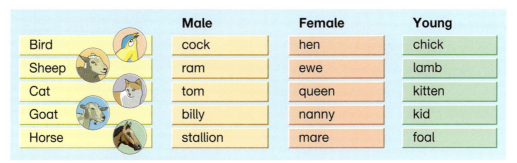

	Male	Female	Young
Bird	cock	hen	chick
Sheep	ram	ewe	lamb
Cat	tom	queen	kitten
Goat	billy	nanny	kid
Horse	stallion	mare	foal

1 You may sometimes be called a kid. Which other creature also has a kid for its young?
2 What is the name of a female cat?
3 What names are given to the parents of a foal?
4 What is the young of a ram and a ewe called?
5 A chick is the young of what animal?
6 Can you give names of the male, female and young of another animal that you know?

Some pupils come to school by bus. The bus timetable shows what time the bus arrives at different places in town.

Bus timetable	Time of arrival					
The station	7.30	7.45	8.00	8.15	8.30	8.45
Town Hall	7.35	7.50	8.05	8.20	8.35	8.50
Market Square	7.45	8.00	8.15	8.30	8.45	9.00
The school	7.50	8.05	8.20	8.35	8.50	9.05

1 John catches the bus at 7:30 from the station. What time does he get to school?
2 Will John be in time for his piano lesson at 8 o'clock?
3 Alison gets on a bus at the Town Hall at 8:20. What time does she arrive at school?
4 What time does the 8:15 bus from the station reach the Market Square?
5 If Kerry needs to arrive at school by 8:35 which is the latest bus she can catch from the Town Hall?
6 School starts at 9:00. If Winston catches the 8:50 bus from the Town Hall will he be late for school?

Now look back at your work in this lesson.
- Can you use a table where the information is organised in rows and columns?
- Do you start from choosing the column or the row?

⑤ Certain, impossible and uncertain

It has been known for frogs to rain from the sky!
This was possibly due to a freak weather condition.
In a hurricane cars can be thrown about.

Which of the following are you certain will happen?

1 The sun will rise tomorrow even if we do not see it.
2 It will rain tomorrow.
3 After May 31st it will be June 1st.

Is it your birthday tomorrow? Maybe it is. But supposing you did this exercise next week. Which of these statements are certain to be true?

1 Someone in your class has a birthday next week.
2 Someone in your school has a birthday next year.
3 Someone in the world has a birthday today.

Some strange things can happen at times, so think very carefully before you answer these questions.

1 Is it impossible to fly in anything that does not have an engine? Give a reason for your answer.
2 Could you to dive to the bottom of the deepest ocean in the world without any diving equipment? Can you say why?
3 Could someone swim across the Channel to France? Do you know if it's ever been done?

D

Sean said he spotted an alien on the way to school this morning!
Do you believe him? You probably think he is making it up. Or
maybe he's dreaming! Could it be true?

Which of the following is impossible?
1 You will live on the moon one day.
2 If you jump off a cliff with paper wings you will be able to fly.
3 You will be very rich when you are old.
4 Someone in Year 8 will pass their driving test today.
5 Jane's baby brother will be older than her in five years' time.

Which of these things are impossible?
6 A car engine made of wood
7 A sharp knife blade made with stone
8 A tree with red leaves
9 A glass hammer

E

Here are some events that are certain to happen – or are they?
Can you think of any reason why they won't?
1 It will rain one day during the summer term.
2 You will have a meal this evening.
3 You will have a birthday sometime this year.
4 One day the Leaning Tower of Pisa will collapse unless it is
   supported.

F

1 Write down two things that you are certain will happen.
2 Think of two things that are impossible.
3 Write down something you would really like to do but you
   are uncertain whether it will happen.
4 Now think of something that you would rather not do but
   you are pretty certain you will have to.

Now look back at your work in this lesson.
• Can you think of a few things that are certain to happen?
  And other things that are impossible?
• Can you think of things that you are not sure will happen?

⑥ Data skills

Which of the trees in the picture would you say is an average size?

All the people in this picture are roughly the same height.

How many times the height of a person is the average tree?

Brendan made a frequency table to show how many runs he scored in several cricket matches last season.

Matches	Number of runs
1st	25
2nd	15
3rd	10
4th	34
5th	15
6th	0
7th	8
8th	15
9th	48

1 How many runs did he score in his first match?

2 In how many matches did he score 15 runs?

3 What was his best score of the season?

4 Did he fail to score in any of his matches?

5 Would you say Brendan was a good player? Give a reason for your answer.

Look at this calendar.

1 How many days does March have?

2 On what day of the week is March the first this year?

3 What are the dates of all the Mondays?

4 Jim's birthday is on the first Saturday in March. What date is this?

5 Asif's birthday is one week later. What is the date of Asif's birthday?

Here is a one set diagram of the pupils in Ken's group. The left-handed pupils are shown in the inner ring.

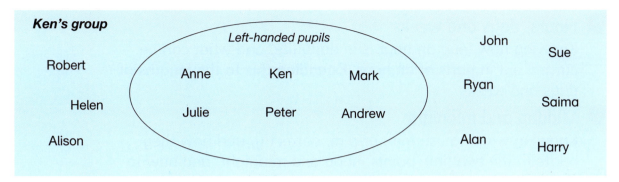

1 How many girls in Ken's group are left-handed?
2 How many boys write with their right hand?
3 Are there more left-handed girls or left-handed boys?
4 How many pupils are in the group?

Look at the following statements.

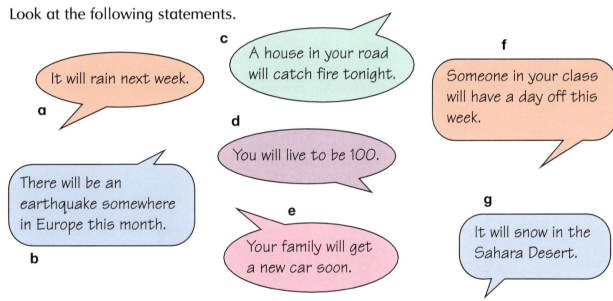

1 Which do you think is the most likely to happen?
2 Can you be certain that it will happen or could something prevent it?
3 Is one of these statements very likely to come true?
4 Which events are unlikely to happen?
5 Are there any statements which are impossible?

Now look back at your work in this lesson.
* Which is easier for you: reading tables or working out whether something is impossible or likely to happen?
* Which mathematical words in this lesson do you understand better than before?

Module **B**7

Number and time measures

1 Hours, days and weeks

Knowing how long an hour is in daily life, and what can be carried out in parts of an hour. Extending this to the lengths of days and weeks

2 Midday and midnight

Knowing when to use a.m. or p.m. correctly, and how they relate to the two time points, noon and midnight, and how to show them on a timeline of the 24 hour day

3 Stopclock

Reading and understanding the different stopwatches and kitchen timers in everyday use. To read the digital and pointer timers

4 Seconds and minutes

Knowing and using the fact that there are 60 seconds in one minute, and being able to change from minutes to seconds and reverse the process

5 Duration in hours

Understanding the duration of time, based on how long daily activities in school, at home and playing games take. Being able to use a timeline to assist calculation

6 Time skills

Revising and practising skills gained in this module

Key words and phrases

midday
midnight
stopclock
timeline

a.m./p.m.
duration
parts of hour
parts of minute

24-hour clock
one-hand clock
clockface
digital display
pointer

① Hours, days and weeks

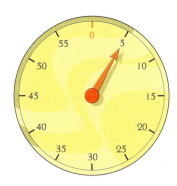

This health pool has a one-hour, one-hand clock. You shouldn't stay in for much longer than one hour in the pool. But you should stay in for at least for half an hour to have enough exercise. Why do you think there are such rules in this health pool? How does the clock help people know how long they have been in the pool?

1 What do you do that normally lasts about one hour?
2 What do you do that normally lasts about half an hour?
3 What takes quarter of an hour?
4 Trace this one-hour clock and mark its centre.

The whole circle represents one hour. How many minutes is that?

5 Cut the circle out. Fold the circle in half making sure the fold passes through the centre.

How many minutes does half a circle represent?

6 Take half the circle and fold it in half again. How many minutes does this represent?
7 How many minutes in 1 1/4 hours?
8 How many minutes in 1 3/4 hours?

1 Copy and complete this fact box.

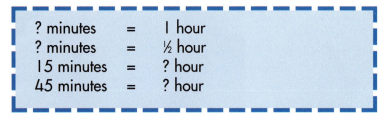

? minutes   =   1 hour
? minutes   =   ½ hour
15 minutes   =   ? hour
45 minutes   =   ? hour

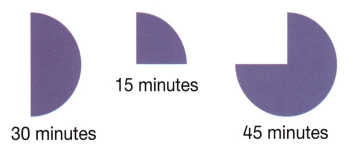

30 minutes   15 minutes   45 minutes

2 Imagine one hand of the clock is at the 5 minutes' mark. Find out what the time will be after half an hour (30 minutes). Use your half circle to make sure. Now find half an hour after the:

3 10 minutes' mark

4 20 minutes' mark

5 30 minutes' mark

6 15 minutes' mark

7 25 minutes' mark

Imagine the hours on the clockface have been stretched out into a line.

There are 12 hours in the line and each hour is split into halves and quarters.

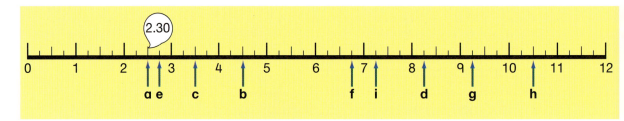

Write down the times marked with letters in the way **a** is written.

Copy the 12 hour line with markers. Label, with an arrow, where these times would be on the line.

1 half-past ten

2 quarter past nine

3 quarter to nine

4 half-past five

5 quarter to two

6 quarter past one

7 half-past eight

8 quarter to eleven

60 minutes	=	1 hour
24 hours	=	1 day
7 days	=	1 week

How many minutes in these times?

1 3 hours

2 two and a half hours

3 6 hours

How many hours in the following?

4 2 days

5 10 days

6 5 days

How many days in the following?

7 2 weeks

8 4 weeks

9 10 weeks

Can you solve these problems?

1 Tammy booked a holiday for two weeks. How many days is this?

2 Richard is going on a football tour for 21 days. How many weeks is this?

3 Abdul takes four weeks to complete his design technology project. How many days did it last?

4 Susan is visiting her Grandma for a day. How many hours is this?

5 Emma is spending two days travelling to Scotland. How many hours is this?

6 Ben takes 72 hours to repair his motorbike. How many days is this?

7 Sasha looks at her watch. The time reads 7:05. Her friend is due to arrive in half an hour. What time is she coming?

8 Nathan has to be at school 9:00 which is in 3/4 hour. What time is it now?

Now look back at your work in this lesson.
- Think of four things that take more than one hour to do, and four things that take half an hour to do.
- Do you know how long a week is and how many hours there are in a full day and night?

② Midday and midnight

Before the clocks were invented, people told the time by the sun. The shortest shadow happens at exactly at midday. Why is midday useful for people to tell the time?

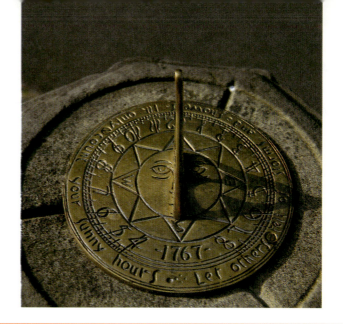

Think about time.

1 What time do you wake up in the morning?
2 At what time of day do you eat your lunch?
3 Lunchtime is between morning and afternoon. What time of day do we call this?
4 What do we call the middle of the night?

> If we are talking about an event that happens before midday we write **a.m.** which comes from the Latin for 'before midday'.
> If an event happens after midday we write **p.m.** which comes from the Latin for 'after midday'.

5 Make a list of three things you do before lunch and three things you do after lunch. Write next to them a.m. or p.m.

Copy the double 12 hour timeline on a strip of tracing paper, and stick in it your book. Where the timeline goes over the edge you need to fold it back neatly.

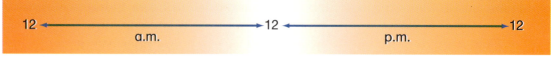

Colour the timeline to show when:
1 You are asleep (blue)
2 You are awake (yellow)

Mark and label with an arrow the times that:
3 You get up
4 You go to school
5 The beginning of lunchtime
6 When school finishes
7 You start your homework
8 The time that you go to bed

C

a.m. is the time from midnight until midday.
p.m. is the time from midday until midnight.

Say whether these times are a.m. or p.m.
1 You catch the bus to go to school.
2 You eat fish and chips for tea.
3 The school team plays netball after school.
4 You get up and wash before breakfast.
5 You arrive home after a disco.
6 You clean your teeth before going to bed.
7 Your form tutor takes the morning register.

D

State whether the pictures show an event happening in the morning (a.m.) or in the afternoon or evening (p.m.)

Use your timeline to decide whether these events are a.m. or p.m.

Make up a time of your own for each event and write next to the time whether it is a.m. or p.m.

Now look back at your work in this lesson.
- Do you know what a.m. and p.m. mean?
- Do you know why midday and midnight are important?

❸ Stopclock

Championship chess uses two clocks. Each player can only take half an hour of his own time to do 20 moves, otherwise he loses. After a move, the player stops his clock which automatically starts the other player's clock.

Answer the following questions.

1 Press the start button on the stopwatch and let it rotate through one full turn. Press the same button again to stop the pointer. Now press the reset button to begin again. Try this a few times to become familiar with the buttons.

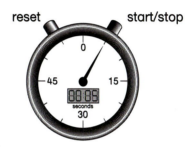

2 Look at the stopwatch. When the pointer rotates through one full circle, how many seconds have passed?

3 How many seconds do you think are in one minute?

4 What would the digital display show when the pointer has made one full turn?

a

b

c

5 Look at the displays above. Which number is the hand pointing to?

6 Write the numbers as a digital display.

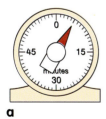
a

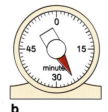
b

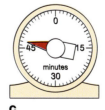
c

7 Look at these kitchen timers. Think about the number of spaces between each big mark. Which number is the pointer showing?

What does each small division on these timers represent?
Write the number of seconds/minutes each timer is pointing to.

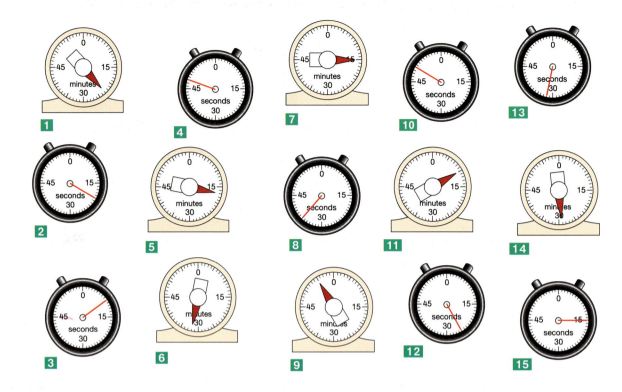

Use this template to draw a stopclock for each of these questions.
Place your pointer to represent these times.

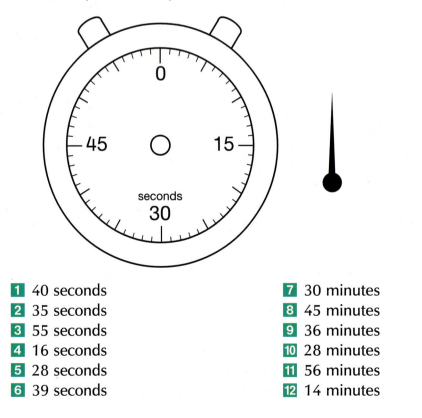

1 40 seconds
2 35 seconds
3 55 seconds
4 16 seconds
5 28 seconds
6 39 seconds

7 30 minutes
8 45 minutes
9 36 minutes
10 28 minutes
11 56 minutes
12 14 minutes

With a partner, use a stopwatch to do the following time trials.
Record your results, in a table like the one below. The first person
should time the second person doing the activity. Then swap jobs.

Results table	First person	Second person

1 Undoing the laces of the your shoes and then tying them up
   again
2 Writing your full name 20 times
3 Running your fingers all the way around the edge of your
   desk 10 times
4 Using squared grid paper draw ten squares
5 Stretching your arms fully to the front then folding and
   stretching your fingers 50 times

Write down the digital times in seconds that these clocks are
showing.

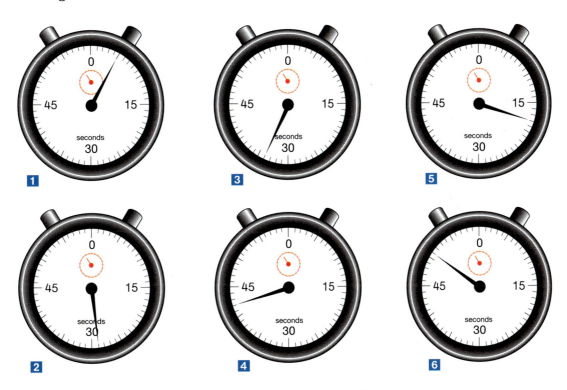

Look at the pointer carefully each time, and count the spaces,
before writing your answer.

Now look back at your work in this lesson.
 • Can you use a dial stopwatch?
 • Can you use a dial kitchen timer as well as a digital one?

④ Seconds and minutes

Trained divers can hold their breath under water for a few minutes. Most people can stay under water for many seconds.

To know how many seconds you are under water some people start counting from 21 up. Why not start from 1? If you counted from 21 to 121, how many seconds would you have stayed underwater? How many minutes?

These times are gives in seconds. Work out how many minutes and seconds there are in each answer.
1 56 + 24 =
2 43 + 36 =
3 42 + 57 =

Now do these subtraction sums of seconds. Give your answer in minutes and seconds, if possible.
4 115 - 60 =
5 87 - 60 =
6 106 - 60 =
7 Write out your 6 times table.

Use your 6 and 10 times tables to convert minutes to seconds, and seconds to minutes. Remember that 60 is 6 times 10.
8 How many seconds in three minutes?
9 How many minutes in 120 seconds?
10 How many seconds in five minutes?

> There are 60 seconds in one minute.

These sums are all given in seconds. Add them and say whether your answer is more than one minute or less than one minute.
1 20 + 30
2 45 + 25
3 15 + 25
4 30 + 35
5 29 + 46
6 38 + 16
7 27 + 39
8 18 + 23

C Look at your answers to exercise B. Work out how many minutes, and how many seconds each one is, for each answer that is more than one minute.

To find the answers you have to subtract 60 from the answer you have. Here are some practice questions.

1. 75 - 60
2. 92 - 60
3. 84 - 60
4. 69 - 60

5. 113 - 60
6. 102 - 60
7. 98 - 60
8. 109 - 60

D Six competitors enter a swimming race. The results are shown below.

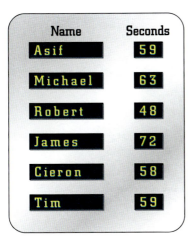

Name	Seconds
Asif	59
Michael	63
Robert	48
James	72
Cieron	58
Tim	59

To qualify to go forward for the county team, the competitors must complete the race in under a minute. Who will qualify? Write the person's name, and the number of seconds next to it.

E

I minute = 60 seconds
1/2 minute = 30 seconds

Find out how many seconds there are in these times.

1. 2 minutes
2. 3 minutes
3. 5 minutes
4. 2 1/2 minutes
5. 4 1/2 minutes
6. 1 1/2 minutes

Now look back at your work in this lesson.
- Can you work out how many minutes there are in numbers of seconds?
- Can you change any number of minutes to seconds only?

⑤ Duration in hours

This man made a record 1000 hours of continuous riding on the Blackpool roller coaster. He stopped for five minutes in each hour and ate and drank on the move. Some people called him a nutter, others a good sportsman. What do you think?

How long is 1000 hours? What is the normal time for a roller coaster ride?

To find the time gap between 4:15 p.m. and 6:00 p.m. use a timeline like this one.

4:15 → 4:30 → 5:00 → 6:00
15 minutes + 30 minutes + 1 hour = 1 hour 45 minutes

How many hours and minutes are there between these times?
1 3:25 a.m. → 5:00 a.m.
2 1:20 p.m. → 3:00 p.m.
3 5:17 p.m. → 6:00 pm
4 8:10 a.m. → 12:30 p.m.

A football match began at 1:45 p.m. They played 45 minutes each way, with an interval of five minutes at half-time.
1 How long was the match, in minutes?
2 Convert this to hours and minutes.
3 What time did the match finish?
4 If you left home to travel to the match at 1:10 p.m. and arrived home at 6:35 p.m. how long would you have been away from the house?

C

Use your timeline to find out how long each programme lasts.

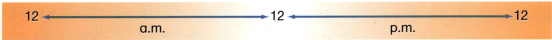

12 ←	→ 12 ←	→ 12
a.m.	p.m.	

If you watch 'Keep Fit Now' and 'Look at Your Diet', how long would you be watching television?

Thursday		
BBC 1		
6.30 a.m. News and Weather	**12.00 p.m.** Tot's Time	**4.30 p.m.** Artscope
7.00 a.m. Breakfast Together	**12.30 p.m.** Children's News	**5.00 p.m.** Local News
7.30 a.m. Keep Fit Now	**1.00 p.m.** Lunchtime Regional News	**5.30 p.m.** Soapland
8.00 a.m. Look at Your Diet	**1.10 p.m.** National News	**6.00 p.m.** National News
9.00 a.m. Today	**2.00 p.m.** Film: The Pirates of the South	**6.15 p.m.** Westenders
10.00 a.m. Schools' programmes		**6.45 p.m.** The Vets

7:30   →   8:00 → 9:00
30 minutes + 1 hour = 1 hour 30 minutes

Calculate how many minutes the following programmes would last.

1 Breakfast Together
2 Schools' programmes

3 Children's News
4 The Film

Which programmes would you be watching at the following times?

5 7 a.m.
6 12:39 p.m.
7 9 a.m.

8 4:30 p.m.
9 7:30 a.m.
10 2 p.m.

D

What period of time would have passed if you watched the following programmes?

1 Tots Time and Children's News
2 Artscope and Soapland
3 Schools' programmes and Tot's Time
4 News and Weather and Breakfast Together
5 Lunchtime Regional News and National News
6 The Pirates of the South, and Artscope

E

1 Andrea went by car from Ashford to Sheffield. She left home at 6:35 a.m. and arrived at 11:00 a.m. How long did the journey take?
2 Robin travelled by train from Ashford to Sheffield. His journey began at 7:45 a.m. and he arrived in Sheffield at 1:35 p.m. How long did the train journey take?
3 Use your answers from questions 1 and 2 to decide which transport was quicker that day.

Now look back at your work in this lesson.
• Can you use a timeline to show how long it takes to do something?
• Which is easier to use: a timeline or numbers on their own?

6 Time skills

What does the science fiction idea of time travel mean? Do you think time travel is really possible? What time would you like to go forward or back to?

1. Write the time that is half an hour after 6:00 p.m.
2. Write the time that is 15 minutes after 5:30 a.m.
3. Write the time that is 45 minutes before 3:00 p.m.
4. What time do you get up during the week?
5. Use a stopwatch to time yourself standing on one leg. Start the stopwatch, then do not look at it. Estimate when 30 seconds have passed, then stop it. Try again to improve your estimation of 30 seconds.
6. Use a kitchen timer or a clock in your classroom to time yourself sitting silently for two minutes. How many seconds is this?

Find 1/2 an hour after each of these times.

Find 15 minutes after each of these times.

Answer the following questions.

1 What time does it get dark at the moment?

2 Write something you could do at 12:30 p.m. on a Saturday.

3 What time is it three hours before noon? Is it p.m. or a.m.?

4 What is the time three hours after midnight? Say if it is a.m. or p.m.

5 At what time of day do you eat your breakfast on a school day?

6 The TV programmes for teenagers begin at five o'clock in the afternoon. Is this a.m. or p.m.?

Eight pupils took part in a competition to copy a paragraph from a book as quickly as possible.

Their teacher timed them and wrote the results in a table.

Name	Seconds	Name	Seconds
Andrew	79	Imran	109
Jason	68	Laura	87
Becky	72	James	99
Fakanda	65	Samantha	94

1 Who finished first?

2 Who took the longest to complete the task?

3 Work out how many minutes and seconds each pupil took. Enter your findings in a table like this one.

Name	Minutes	Seconds	Name	Minutes	Seconds
Andrew			Imran		
Jason			Laura		
Becky			James		
Fakanda			Samantha		

E

Three friends ran in today's race.

Ann
47 seconds

Jean
36 seconds

Emma
58 seconds

Look at the picture above. In the race who came:
1 first
2 second
3 last
4 How many seconds faster did the first come?

F

Answer these questions.
1 Sue went on a charity walk. She took 245 minutes. Change this to hours and minutes.
2 Simon is catching a train. He arrives at the station at 7:15. He has 3/4 of an hour to wait for the train. What time is the train due in?
3 Joseph runs a race in 95 seconds. Convert this to minutes and seconds.
4 I looked at the clock in the middle of the night. At first it read 11:00, later it read 5:43.

Write these times using a.m. and p.m.
5 Nigel goes fishing for 3 hours 20 minutes. Use a calculator to work out how many minutes this is altogether, and then change this into seconds.
6 Show many hours and minutes have passed between 12:19 a.m. to 6:20 a.m.
7 Show many hours and minutes have passed between 3:56 p.m. to 7:30 p.m.

Now look back at your work in this lesson.
• Have you improved your skills in changing minutes to seconds and from seconds to minutes?
• Which mathematical words in this lesson do you understand better than before?

Module B8

Shape and space

1 Main shapes

Recognising 2D shapes, naming them and distinguishing them from each other by properties such as the number and equality of sides, ignoring the issue of size

2 Sorting shapes

Sorting 2D shapes in various rules, normally in two sets. This conforms to the level of work in handling data

3 Sorting solids

Recognising the difference between 2D and 3D shapes. Sorting 3D objects by recognising differences between them and intuitive knowledge of their properties

4 Shapes on the grid

Using grids to copy components of shapes, by locating points in relation to each other using counts of units and direction

5 Turning shapes around

Recognising the effect of turning a shape or a combination of a line and a shape around in producing a symmetrical shape with rotation order 4

6 Skills with shapes

Reinforcing recognition and sorting of 2D and 3D shapes. Consolidating work covered in this module.

Key words and phrases

2D shapes
3D shapes or solid objects
grouping shapes
sorting shapes

flat shapes
sides of a rectangle
number of sides
rotation order 4
three dimensions: length, width, height

area
grid
line on a grid
square grid paper
straight across to left or right
straight down or up
vertical

❶ Main shapes

Abstract artists often use different shapes to show things in their paintings. This is an artist's view of a shield.

A

1 How many shapes are there with four sides in this picture?
2 How many circles can you find?
3 How many shapes are there with three sides?
4 Look at the shapes with four sides. Write how many shapes have two long sides and two short sides.
5 Look around your classroom and make a list of any objects that are similar in shape to those in the pattern you have been studying.

Rectangles

• Rectangles always have 4 sides – 2 long sides of equal length, and 2 shorter sides of equal length.
• Another word for a rectangle is 'oblong'.

Squares

• Squares always have 4 sides. The sides are always equal lengths.
• In maths, a square is a special kind of rectangle.

B

Look at these shapes.

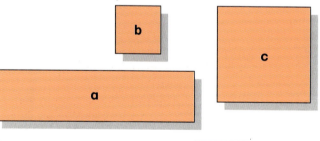

1 Which shapes are square?
2 Which shapes are oblong?
3 Which is the biggest square?
4 Which is the smallest oblong?
5 Make a list of the squares, in order of size, starting with the biggest first.
6 Make a list of the oblongs, in order of size, starting with the smallest first.

C

Look at these shapes.

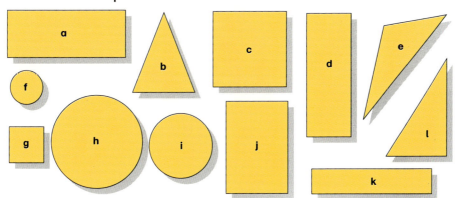

1 **a** and **d** are oblongs. Find one more.
2 **b** and **e** are triangles. Find another.
3 Name the shapes **c** and **g**.
4 Name the shapes **f** and **h**.

D

Triangles always have three sides. The sides do not have to be the same length.

1 Draw the road signs that are in triangles.
2 The other road signs are in circles. Trace or copy these.

E

Use these words to describe the shapes you can see in the picture.

triangle square oblong circle (round)

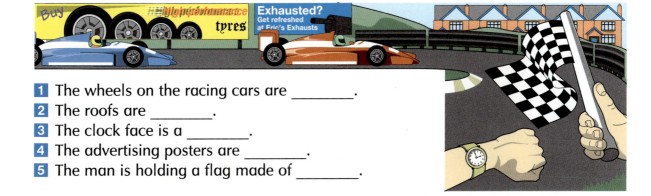

1 The wheels on the racing cars are _____.
2 The roofs are _____.
3 The clock face is a _____.
4 The advertising posters are _____.
5 The man is holding a flag made of _____.

Now look back at your work in this lesson.
• How many regular shapes do you know?
• How do you know which is which?

2 Sorting shapes

The streets in Hong Kong are lit up at night with all kinds of signs. There are regular shapes in bus windows and shop signs.

1 Count all the regular shapes you see in the picture.
2 How many squares can you see?
3 Are the oblongs all the same size?
4 Are there any shapes with more than four sides? Draw the shapes you have found or trace them.
5 Beside each of your shapes write how many sides it has.
6 What do you call the shapes with three sides?

Sort these shapes into two groups.

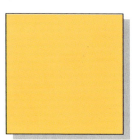

Copy the shapes into group A and group B.

Group A Shapes with three sides	Group B Shapes with four sides

Look at these shapes. Sort these shapes into two groups. Choose
your own rule.

1 Draw two boxes like the ones below. Now copy the shapes
into the boxes.

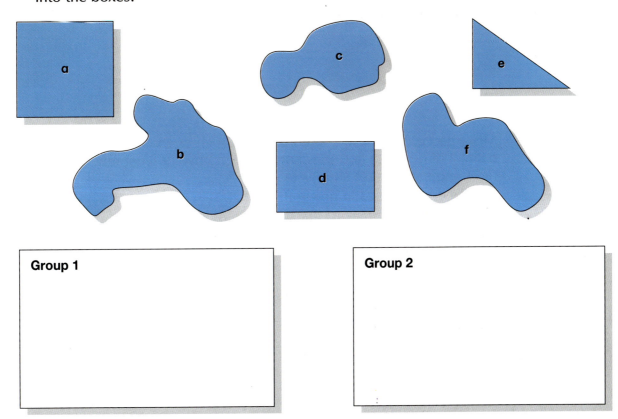

Group 1	Group 2

2 Write a sentence to explain how you decided which group
to put each shape in.

Sort these shapes into three groups.

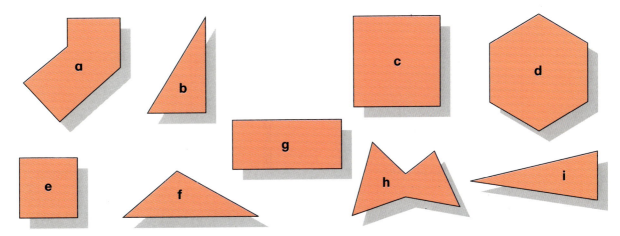

1 Write down the shapes with three sides.
2 Write down the shapes with four sides.
3 Write down the shapes with six sides.

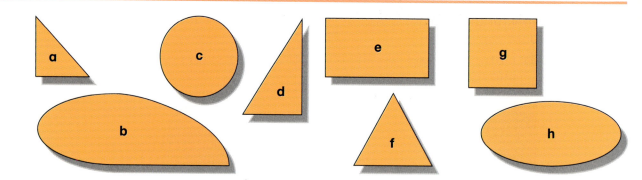

1 Make two groups. Use a square corner such as the corner of a sheet of paper to find the shapes which have at least one right angle. Put these shapes in group A.
Put the other shapes in group B.

2 Write down the names of the shapes in group A.

Group A	Group B

Make two groups. Draw some shapes of your own and put them into the correct group.

Group A Curved sides	**Group B** Straight sides

Now look back at your work in this lesson.
- Can you sort shapes into sets?
- What rules do you use when sorting shapes: number of sides or just colour and size?

③ Sorting solids

People say we live in a 3D world.
What does that mean?
What words are there to describe
the three dimensions?
Can you find two different sets in
this collection?

For this exercise you will need to work as a whole class or in
groups. There should be at least two solid shapes per person.

> • These shapes all have six faces, and eight corners.
> • They are called cuboids. A cube is a special kind of cuboid.

1 In turns, each person picks up two shapes to turn around in
their hands.
2 Describe what is different and what is the same between the
two shapes to the pupils in your group.

Look at these shapes.

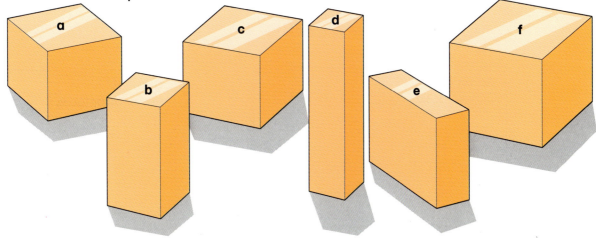

1 Sort these shapes into two groups.
2 How did you decide which group to put the shapes in?
3 Describe the shape of the faces. How many are there?

Put these shapes in two groups.

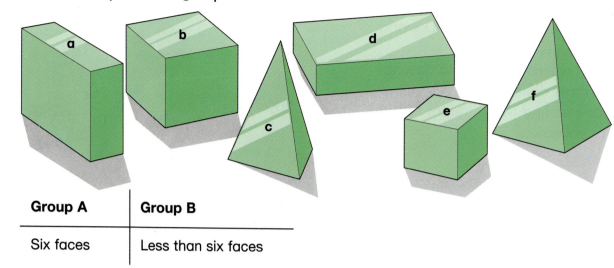

Group A	Group B
Six faces	Less than six faces

1 Describe the shapes in each group.
2 Could you arrange these shapes into three groups?
3 How have you made up each group?

Here are some more shapes.

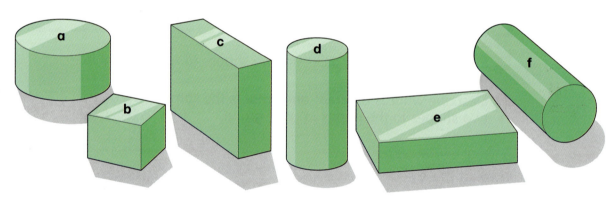

1 Put these shapes into two groups.

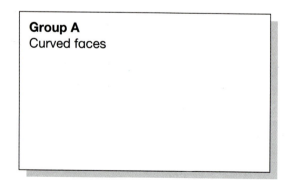

Group A
Curved faces

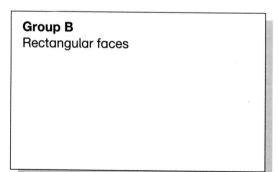

Group B
Rectangular faces

2 What things in real life are nearly or exactly the same shape as group A? Can you name one or two things?
3 What things are like the shapes in group B?

E

These shapes have been sorted into two groups.

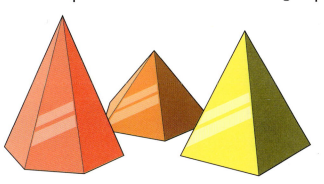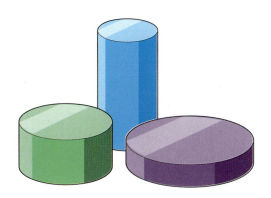

1 Describe the way they have been sorted.
2 Can you think of something that looks like a pyramid?

F

Now look at these shapes.

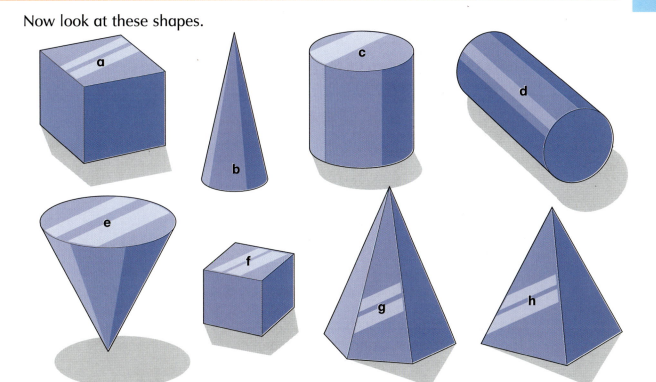

1 Sort these shapes into four groups A–D.
2 Use these words to describe the groups you have made.

face	pointed	square	curved	triangles	corners	oblong

3 Write a sentence to describe each group.

Now look back at your work in this lesson.
- Do you know the difference between a 2D shape and a 3D shape?
- What does the letter D stand for in 2D and 3D?

4 Shapes on the grid

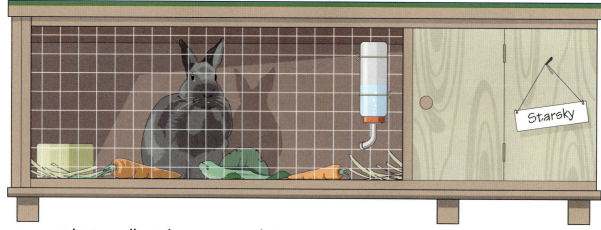

What is a grid? Are all grids square grids?
You can copy shapes on square grids easily. Why?

 Look at the lines drawn on these grids. You can measure them by counting the squares.

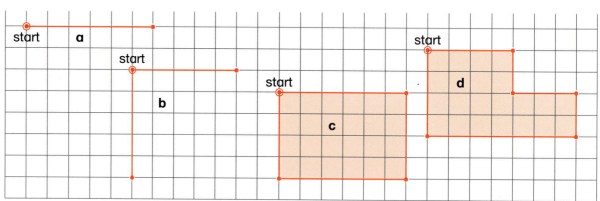

1 Look at shape **a**. Which of these is true?
The line is drawn straight across to the left.
The line is drawn straight down.
The line is drawn straight across to the right.
The line is drawn straight up.
2 Draw the line in shape **a** on grid paper.
3 Look at shape **b**. How long is the line drawn to the right?
4 How long is the line drawn down?
5 Do the two lines in shape **b** look the same length to you?
6 Draw the shape **b** on grid paper.
7 What is the name of shape **c**?
8 How long is the longer side?
9 What is the length of the shorter side?
10 Draw the shape on your grid paper.
11 How many sides has shape **d**?
12 How many corners has shape **d**?
13 Copy shape **d** on your grid paper.

Look at the lines drawn on these grids.

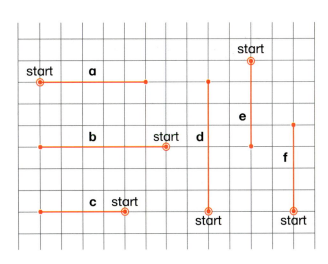

For each line on this grid write down how long it is and the direction you draw it from Start. For example, line **a** is five units across to the right.

Copy the six lines on your grid paper.

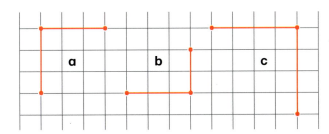

Copy the three shapes on your grid paper.

Look at the lines drawn on these grids.

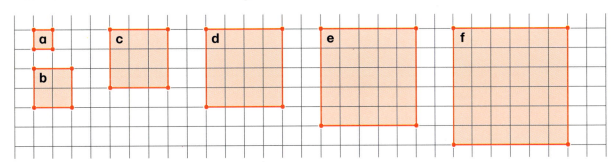

Copy the squares on to your grid paper.
Write the length of the sides on each shape.
How many squares are inside each shape?
Copy and complete the table below with your answers to these questions.

Grid	Number of squares along	Number of squares down	Number of squares inside
a			
b			
c			
d			
e			
f			

What is the space inside a shape called?

Shape and space

119

Look at the lines drawn on these grids.

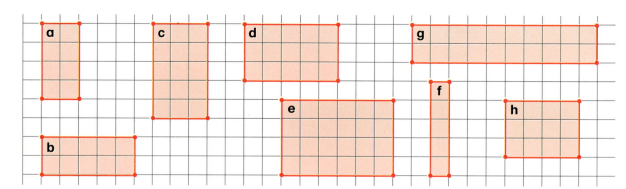

1 Copy the eight rectangles on your grid paper.
2 Are any two rectangles the same?
3 Find out how many squares are inside each shape.
4 Copy the table to record your results.

Grid	Number of squares
a	
b	
c	
d	
e	
f	
g	
h	

Look at the lines drawn on these grids.

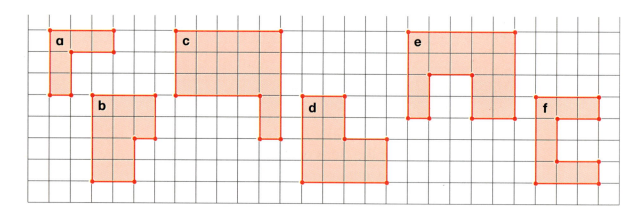

1 Copy these shapes on your grid paper.
2 Find each shape's area (how many squares inside) and write that next to it.

Now look back at your work in this lesson.
• Can you use a grid to copy shapes?
• How do you know how long each line is when you copy shapes on a grid?

⑤ Turning shapes around

How many people can you see on this side of the fairground ride? Do you think the ride is symmetrical? Why not?

 Follow these directions.

1 Draw a cross. Make sure the angles are right angles.
2 Find a small square of card or a die. Draw round this to put a square at the top of your cross.
3 Now put a square on the ends of the other three lines of the cross.
4 Using a piece of tracing paper, trace one line and its square. Turn the tracing paper around the middle point. Does the square fit all the squares?

> We call this rotation symmetry order 4.

5 What is another word for 'rotation'?
6 What is another word for 'symmetry'?
7 What does 'order 4' mean?

 Follow these directions.

1 Draw two lines to make a cross. Check that the lines cross at right angles.
2 Cut a small triangle from card to use as a template, or find a triangle to draw around.
3 Use your small triangle to copy the design above. Make sure you put the triangle lying on the same side each time.
4 Complete this design to finish the rotation.

Follow these directions.

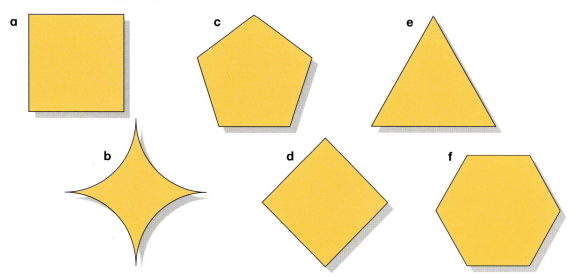

1 Trace square **a** on tracing paper. Then mark the middle of the square with a dot.

2 Write the first letter of your name in the top left corner of the square, on the tracing paper.

3 Keep your tracing square on top of the textbook square and put a pen on the middle point.

4 Turn your tracing paper till your letter goes into the top right corner of the book square. Then turn your paper again.

5 How many times does your letter fit around the square?

6 Which other shapes have a rotation order 4?

Can you draw some more of your own?

Follow Steps 1–4 to see how this design was drawn. Complete the design by drawing Step 5.

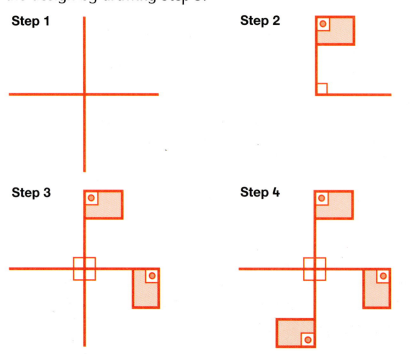

E Here are some more designs. Copy and complete to show rotation order 4.

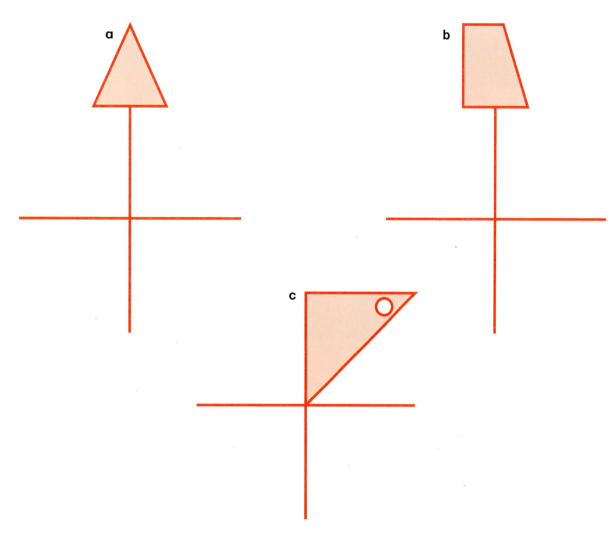

1 Draw a cross on your paper. Take a small piece of card and cut out a shape of your own.
2 Place your shape on the vertical line of the cross, near the top, and draw round it.
3 Continue around the cross, drawing round the shape, in the same position on each of the lines. Remember the one at the bottom will be upside down. It may help you to turn your paper as you move to the next point.
4 Copy one of the designs below. Draw a face in the shape. Continue this design to give rotation order 4.

Now look back at your work in this lesson.
• Do you know what rotation means?
• Can you think of shapes other than those in this lesson which have a rotation symmetry?

⑥ Skills with shapes

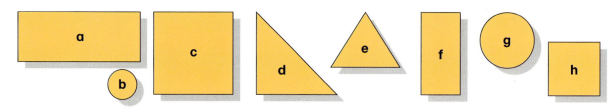

Airplane pilots see different shapes as they fly over cities and countryside.
What shapes would you see if you flew over your home?

A Look at these shapes.

1. Name the shapes that have four right angles. Use a square corner to identify and check these.
2. Name the shapes that only have three corners.
3. Which shapes are round?
4. Draw a rectangle and a square.
5. Write the name of shapes **d** and **e**.
6. Pick words from this box to help you complete this sentence.

| straight | round | not | pointed |

Circles are _____, and they do _____ have any corners.

B Look at these shapes.

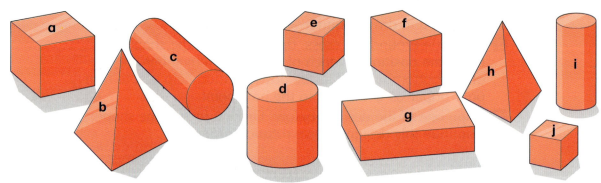

1. Sort these 3D shapes into groups:
   Shapes that have six faces
   Shapes that are made up from triangles
   Shapes that have a curved face
2. Sketch a solid shape that has all square faces.

Look at these shapes.

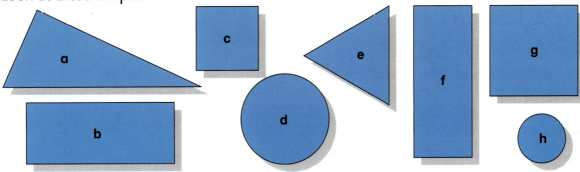

C

1 How many oblongs can you see?

2 Draw a large oblong with a small square inside it. Colour the square red. Colour the rest of the rectangle green.

3 Using cm² paper make a pattern using squares and oblongs. Remember that squares have sides of all the same length, oblongs have two longer sides and two shorter sides.

4 Colour the squares in one colour, and the oblongs in another.

5 Use a pair of compasses, or a pin and measured length of card, to draw three circles of different sizes.

6 Shade in the biggest circle. Use your ruler to make stripes on the smallest circle.

Look at the picture.

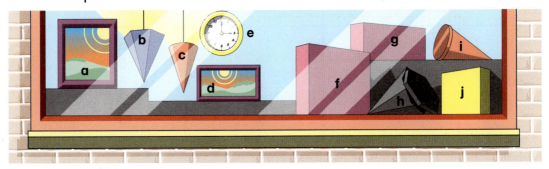

D

1 Write down the names of the flat shapes that are round.

2 What is the shape of the pictures?

3 Could you have a picture that is any other shape? Name these shapes.

4 Match the shapes with the boxes that they would fit into. Write the letters of the shape and box that go together.

Now look back at your work in this lesson.
- Can you sort shapes and solid objects by the number of sides or faces each one has?
- Which mathematical words in this lesson do you understand better than before?

Module B5–B8

Practise your skills

Number and algebra

Write the answers to these questions by working them out in your head.

1 56 - 10 =

2 75 - 10 - 5 - 2 =

3 76 - 10 - 2 - 2 - 2 =

Put these numbers in order of largest first.

4 128, 126, 124, 117, 139, 125

5 989, 999, 987, 890, 962, 998

Handling data

Five members of a school's fishing club recorded their catch over one week in season in three popular spots. This is the table they produced.

Name	Grand Lake	Inn Pond	Holly Stream
Avrill	2	11	5
Paul	5	6	8
Mohammed	10	2	6
Rhoda	4	0	7
Mitch	7	5	8

1 How many fish did Paul catch at Holly Stream?

2 Who caught more fish at Inn Pond?

3 How many fish did Mitch catch altogether?

4 How many fish did all the pupils catch at Grand Lake?

5 Who caught more fish: Mohammed or Paul?

Number and time measures

1. Write the time that is half an hour after 7:30 a.m.
2. Write the time that is 15 minutes after 7:30 a.m.
3. Write the time that is 45 minutes before 7:30 a.m.
4. What time will it be six hours after 7:30 a.m.?
5. How many minutes are there in one and a half hours?

Shape and space
Copy these shapes on to cm² paper.

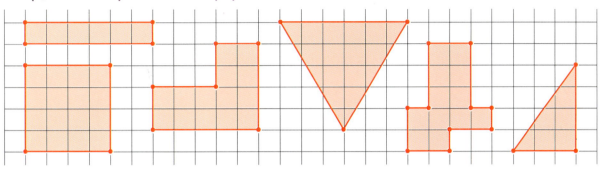

1. Complete rotation order 4. You may cut shapes to use if necessary.
2. On cm² paper draw two oblongs of different sizes. Label them oblongs.
3. Draw three different size squares. Label them squares.
4. Draw four triangles, one with a right angle. Label them triangles.
5. Look around the room. Find a 3D shape that has six faces. Write a few sentences that describe the shape you have found. The words in this box may help you.

| edge | face | corners | square | oblong | right angle |

Now try this...
Use this L-shape to make a puzzle.
Copy the L-shape on transparent paper four or more times.
Cut them out and join them to make a closed shape.

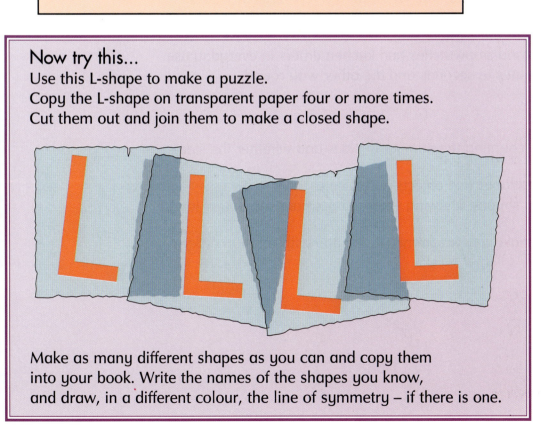

Make as many different shapes as you can and copy them into your book. Write the names of the shapes you know, and draw, in a different colour, the line of symmetry – if there is one.

Check your skills

You can check how well you can do the things listed here. Get your parents and friends to help. Your teacher will give you a copy of this page to tick on.

Number

1 I know how to add numbers such as 30 + 40 together, and how to add 10 to numbers, or take away 10 from numbers, without pencil and paper or calculator. ☐

2 I can work out in my head how to add numbers such as 30, 40 or 70, and so on, to numbers such as 14 and 36. ☐

3 I know which one of two three-digit numbers is bigger and where a thousand comes in the number sequence. ☐

4 I can count in 2s forward or back, and in 5s, and 10s. ☐

5 I know what to do to go back from a position or a number, by doing the opposite action to what has been done before. ☐

Data

1 I can read tables of numbers to answer questions or complete with numbers from a survey. I can read a train timetable. ☐

2 I know roughly what 'average' means. ☐

3 I can sort things by what they have in common. ☐

4 I can understand when things are certain to happen or are impossible and that we cannot be sure about many other things. ☐

Time

1 I know what can take hours to do, and what takes a few days or weeks. ☐

2 I know when to use a.m. or p.m. correctly, and where are noon and midnight on a timeline of the 24 hour day. ☐

3 I can read and understand stopwatches and kitchen timers in everyday use. ☐

4 I can change from minutes to seconds and the other way round. ☐

Shape and space

1 I can name shapes by counting the number of sides and whether the sides are equal or not. ☐

2 I can sort 2D and 3D shapes and objects in two sets. ☐

3 I can use grids to copy shapes, knowing where to put points and how long the lines are. ☐

4 I can turn a shape to make a new symmetrical shape with rotation order 4. ☐